Free to Be

A PATHWAY TO
INNER LIBERATION

Kim Gross

Finn-Phyllis
Press

Copyright © 2024 by Kim Gross

Published by Finn-Phyllis Press
Phoenix, AZ

All rights reserved. No part of this publication may be reproduced, distributed or transmitted in any form or by any means, including photocopying, recording, or other electronic or mechanical methods, without the prior written permission of the publisher, except in the case of brief quotations embodied in critical reviews and certain other noncommercial uses permitted by copyright law.

Free to Be / Kim Gross —1st ed.

Library of Congress Control Number: 2024918684
ISBN 979-8-9905359-3-0 (pbk)
ISBN 979-8-9905359-4-7 (eBook)

PRAISE FOR FREE TO BE

"Free to Be takes us on a transformative journey from people-pleasing and perfectionism to personal liberation. Kim masterfully blends memoir and self-help, weaving important lessons with relatable stories that offer deep insights into the patterns holding us back from our true selves. She illuminates the path from a guarded heart and unhealed pain to the paradise of authenticity and self-love. Kim's vulnerable, inspiring storytelling makes this book a joy to read, tracing her evolution from childhood through parenthood to her liberated, true self. Offering a map to personal freedom, improved relationships, and deeper connections, it's a must-read for anyone struggling with people-pleasing and perfectionism. Kim provides both self-compassion for past experiences and hope for a new way forward. Her inspirational teaching and honest sharing will leave readers feeling understood and empowered to embrace their authentic selves. Don't miss this opportunity to become free to be your true self."

—Deb Blum, Sacred Marriage Transformation Guide for Midlife Moms

"A thought-provoking and insightful read for anyone struggling with the belief that they were born "damaged, unloveable, and just not good enough." Kim powerfully takes us through her amazing personal journey of recovery and healing from childhood trauma to finding her "true self." Her style of teaching insightfully and effectively weaves her personal story with the notion that people live out patterns of behavior and hide behind "masks" to protect themselves from abandonment and rejection. Kim's book is a must read for anyone who wants to find their personal power and positive self-esteem and especially for parents raising children."

—**Bob Holtz, M.A., M.B.A., Addiction and Childhood Trauma Therapist**

"Kim candidly shares her personal story and invites all of us to the important conversation that finding true peace and fulfillment is an inside job no matter your external circumstances. I applaud Kim for her courage in taking her own masks off while simultaneously inviting and inspiring others to do the same."

—**Suzanne Stauffer, Soul Coach**

"A powerful guide to help others to identify patterns that we live out, particularly people-pleasing and perfectionism. Kim illustrates through her own journey of living out patterns and not a life, what causes us to have these patterns and how they prevent us from reclaiming our true selves."

—**Dr. Jessica Rabon, PhD Licensed Clinical Psychologist**

"Kim's POWER framework helps others recognize their patterns and take ownership while inviting them to heal their wounds to create the life they desire."

—**Holly Swenson, RN, Award-Winning and Best-Selling Author of** *Stop, Drop, Grow & Glow*

"Kim bravely peels back the layers of her own life, revealing the raw and unfiltered truths that most of us keep hidden. With a heart full of courage and a soul steeped in authenticity, she invites us all to take off our masks and step into our truest selves. Her stories will make you laugh, cry, and see yourself reflected in the most unexpected ways. Kim's words are not just inspiring—they're a call to action for anyone longing to live more openly and genuinely. This book is a testament to the beauty of vulnerability and the strength found in showing up just as you are."

—**Sabrina Victoria, Founder of Her Nation Global**

"Kim bares her soul and her most precious memories with the reader to show you that you, too, have your own power within to heal and learn how to live without the masks you have been so accustomed to in your life. She teaches the reader to be braver than their fear to bring them into a place of wholeness. I recommend this book for anyone on their healing journey. You will feel supported and held in these pages.

—**Janet Philbin, LCSW, Author of** *Show Up For Yourself A Guide to Inner Awareness and Growth*

Contents

Foreword 7

Introduction 11

PART I 23

    Ch 1: How Did I Get Here? 25

    Ch 2: Living Out Patterns 41

    Ch 3: The Masks We Wear 47

PART II 75

    Ch 4: Growing Ourselves Up 77

    Ch 5: Confronting the Truth 87

    Ch 6: Eliminating Stinking Thinking 99

PART III 105

    Ch 7: The Giant Sulk 107

    Ch 8: Understanding Emotional Reactivity 119

PART IV 127

    Ch 9: Reparenting Yourself 129

    Ch 10: Integrating Our Whole Selves 137

PART V 151

    Ch 11: Learning How to Communicate 153

    Ch 12: Getting Comfortable Setting Boundaries 171

    Ch 13: Being True to Yourself 181

Ch 14: Opportunities to Grow 191
PART VI 195
Ch 15: Spreading My Message 197
Ch 16: True Freedom 205
Acknowledgements 213

To my son and daughter. May you always be Free to Be. May you always know your inherent worth and that you matter. You mean the world to me.

"The privilege of a lifetime is *being who you are.*"
—Joseph Campbell

FOREWORD

THIS BOOK IS FOR ANYONE WHO has ever felt unworthy to be their true self. If you have been living out patterns and wearing masks to hide your true self and want to unhook from these, this is a must read.

Before we can change anything in our lives, we must be aware that we are living out patterns. You can't change something you aren't even aware of. This is why people wear masks.

In addition to becoming aware of your patterns and why we all wear masks, you have to take responsibility for making the changes in your life. There is no one out there to rescue you but yourself. Only you can create the life you want. Through her journey, Kim shows exactly how she has done this.

I remember well when Kim came to me around twelve years ago. She was especially desperate to change how she parented. Through the countless online courses that I taught over the years, she enrolled in all of them. This enabled her to begin the healing process.

Kim realized that no one on the outside could

affirm her worth; it had to come from inside herself. To begin this process, the first thing she had to do was grieve her lost self. Only when she was fully ready to embrace her whole self could she experience the fullness of life.

I have witnessed over the years how much Kim has healed and grown. It's wonderful to see when someone takes ownership for creating the change in their lives. She has done a great deal of healing that has allowed her to be in this moment in time sharing her growth journey with you.

This powerful, personal, and vulnerable book offers a roadmap for how you can remove the masks that you wear in order to show up as your authentic self. Through Kim's personal story, she shares what it looks and feels like to wear the masks of people-pleasing and perfectionism. I admire how willing she is to share her journey. By sharing the deep pain she once experienced, she inspires and invites you to do our own healing.

I am thrilled to witness the joy, abundance, peace, and freedom that Kim experiences every day. This book will show you how to experience what she now enjoys.

I am deeply moved by Kim's mission and passion to make a mark on the world by teaching others how to remove their masks. She hopes to share this on an educational level with many teachers, students, and parents. She especially wishes to change the lives of teenagers and young adults.

I highly recommend this book for all seeking to be their most authentic selves.

—Dr. Shefali, clinical psychologist and *NYT* bestselling author of *The Conscious Parent*

INTRODUCTION

IF YOU'VE PICKED UP THIS BOOK, you have a nagging sense that your life isn't working as well as you wish it were. Perhaps your relationships aren't as meaningful as you'd like. Maybe you wish your life had a larger degree of meaning and purpose, the kind that makes you excited to wake up every day.

It's a hard place to be in. On some levels, your life is moving along wonderfully (largely because you work hard to make it look like everything is okay). Even though you accomplish a lot, you feel a void inside, which you attempt to distract yourself from by "tuning out." Some common ways people do this include overeating, over-drinking, spending too much time scrolling on social media, or binge-watching Netflix. You enviously peruse your friends' social media posts, wondering why they seem so happy and have it all together while you feel relatively miserable. You might even feel guilty for feeling this way—after all, your life "isn't that bad." You know you should be grateful; so many people have it far worse. So you push your feelings down and carry on with your "life's-not-that-bad Groundhog-Day existence, but you simply can't shake the feeling that something about your life just doesn't feel quite right.

Your relationships aren't horrible, but they're also not great. Perhaps, you feel resentful of all that you do for others—always there for others when they need you—only to have it not be reciprocated. You don't feel comfortable speaking up, asking others to be there for you when you need support, but then feel bad when others don't support you. This leads to feelings of loneliness; you might even begin to feel depressed. At the very least, you're exhausted from being everything to everyone. You're so busy attending to others' expectations while attempting to meet your own unrealistic expectations to do everything perfectly that you don't even know what it looks like to be true to yourself.

You may also feel an emptiness inside, because you have dreams you no longer chase because you're afraid to go for them, so fearful of failure that you play it safe and stick to things that are comfortable. But there is an ache inside you that wants you to expand into the best version of yourself. You think, "If only I had the courage to do what so-and-so is doing. If only I had what it takes to pursue my dreams." But rather than break through the fear, you stay where you are—safe, yet feeling an ache inside because you aren't pursuing your dreams.

I know these feelings well. I often remark that, over the last several years, I've gone from prison to paradise. I'm referring to a prison of the mental variety, of course, one in which I was a victim of my thoughts, beliefs, and patterns. When I lived there, I was attached to external validation. I needed to feel seen and heard and know that I mattered, and I was desperate for others' approval. I also longed to be able to speak up for myself and advocate for my needs without the fear of being rejected. To feel free to be myself without worrying about what others thought. I was exhausted from trying to be everything to everyone, rarely paying attention to my own needs. I could barely *set* a boundary let alone hold any I attempted to make.

I didn't know how to soothe myself or regulate my nervous system, causing me to live in fear most of the time. I put enormous pressure on myself to be perfect, and I set the bar extremely high, for both myself and others. This, in turn, impacted all of my relationships. I longed for others to take care of my emotional needs and simultaneously struggled to believe in myself, which prevented me from stepping outside my comfort zone. All of these thoughts and worries left me feeling like a victim—like I was in the aforementioned mental prison.

Paradise, on the other hand, is freedom from that prison. Paradise is knowing that I am no longer attached to what others think of me. I no longer scour the earth for praise and approval. Paradise is knowing that I can be one hundred percent myself, unapologetically. Paradise is knowing that it is my birthright to show up in the world as myself. To share my thoughts, beliefs, and feelings while no longer being afraid of rejection or abandonment. Paradise is having the ability to connect with others without pretending to be someone I'm not. To have the other accept me for who I am, not who they want me to be, which is the cornerstone of true connection.

Paradise allows for more meaningful relationships, because I feel confident setting boundaries with clear and direct communication. I'm able to have more realistic expectations for myself and accept that my best is good enough. I have more compassion for myself when I make mistakes or fall short of a goal. I take risks to speak up and assert myself, because I am no longer attached to another's approval.

TRUE BELONGING

We all have an innate need to know we are worthy of being loved and accepted for exactly who we are. When we were toddlers, we didn't worry about what others thought of us. If we had mashed carrots all over our face or vomit down our brand-new top, we didn't think to ourselves, "Oh my goodness, what will others think of me?" We were comfortable being our true selves. We knew how to live in the moment and be curious about life. There was no shame in our game.

As adults, many of us want to return to living in that state of child-like wonder, a time when we knew what it was like to be truly present without concern for what others might think. Without transforming ourselves to please others or meet their expectations. We long to once again feel connected to something greater than ourselves. I like to refer to this as our essence, true self, true nature, inner self, or whole self. All of these terms are interchangeable. It is when we are being our true selves that we know we belong in the truest sense.

Brené Brown beautifully explains the difference between belonging and fitting in. *"The thing is that we are wired to be a part of something bigger than us so deeply, that sometimes we will take fitting in as a substitute, but actually fitting in is the greatest barrier to belonging because fitting in says, 'Be like them to be accepted.' Belonging says, 'This is who I am. I hope we can make a connection."*

Fitting in is what we *think* we need to do as we get older, but in our younger years, we didn't think about fitting in. We didn't need to. We innately knew we belonged, meaning that we knew we were created from the same Source that created the entire universe, and for that reason we are meant to be here. We are worthy of being alive and being our true selves.

There was a time before the age of ten when I knew exactly what it felt like to be calm and peaceful inside myself. During this time in my life, I was heavily connected to nature, and it was during those moments, co-existing with nature, when I felt most comfortable being my true self.

I recall spending summers at my aunt and uncle's

lake house when I was younger. I spent every summer there from age five to seventeen, and it's one of the most beautiful places I have ever been, mostly because of the way I felt when I was there. The day after school let out for the summer, my mom drove me straight there, because I couldn't wait another day to arrive. I stayed until just before school started again, absorbing every last drop of feeling free to be myself.

During these months every year, I felt free to be my truest self, even though I didn't realize that feeling was the basis for the intense joy and peace I had at the time. I would take the rowboat out early in the mornings when the lake was so still, I could see my reflection in the water. I remember putting the oars in the water, one at a time, watching the ripples form. I felt so present, so still, knowing I was a part of something larger than myself. Although I didn't have the language for this feeling as a young girl, what I was experiencing in those moments was my essence, my true nature. Some might say it felt like being intimately connected to a Higher Power, God, or a Higher Self.

That memory reminds me of the stillness I felt at various other times during my childhood when deeply immersed in a moment, as if nothing else existed. I felt it every time I made a snow angel or played in the crisp autumn leaves. In those moments, I felt like I belonged. Even though I was all by myself, I belonged to everything around me. I knew what it meant to love myself for who I was, unconditionally. As a result, I didn't question my worthiness. I inherently knew I was worthy of love and belonging in those moments; I felt connected to the Source that created me.

Over the years, I slowly began to lose touch with that young, free, innocent girl. I began to feel separate and, in many ways and many instances, alone. To get back that sense of belonging I craved, I'd often go to extremes to please others and ensure I was doing things the "right" way. I grew up continuing to believe this was necessary: to feel like I belonged, I needed to please others, who would in turn validate that I belonged, that I was worthy of belonging. To please others, I needed to perform well and work hard to make others happy. So, needless to say, I developed strong people-pleasing and perfectionism tendencies. Some of us have such a strong need to belong that we end up dimming or outright hiding our identity, our needs and desires, in order to be accepted. I found it excruciatingly painful to be criticized, rejected, abandoned, concluding that such a response confirmed that I was inadequate and unlovable for who I truly am. It has been a long and painful journey to heal myself from these tendencies, but it's been so worth it, because I have now found my way back to my true self. Where the only person to whom I feel a deep desire to belong is me.

Some people have a pivotal experience, an *aha* moment, a spontaneous awakening that gets them to this point. My journey was different. I peeled back layer after layer of the metaphorical onion over the years. I would go through a period of intense pain while working through and healing a specific layer. Then, after a reprieve, I'd be confronted by another layer. I healed, layer by layer, by working with therapists, reading books, attending twelve-step meetings, and meditating. In essence, I compiled my own toolbox of sorts over time. Eventually, I reached a tipping point where the way I walked through life had significantly shifted. We all, myself included, often want a quick fix. Few people look forward to feeling pain. But the beauty of a gradual journey is that while it can be long and hard, it's also deeper and, therefore, longer lasting.

While there wasn't a single defining moment that caused me to immediately pivot my approach to life, there were two significant events that served as catalysts to wake me up. The first was when I was diagnosed with Sjogren's syndrome, which is a chronic autoimmune disorder. My kids were five and two at the time, and because I was sick and unable to care for them in the way they needed, I knew I had to start taking better care of myself. This led me to develop a self-care practice, including exercise, eating healthier and taking time to rest when I needed it. The second event was attending a talk where Dr. Shefali, a renowned clinical psychologist with expertise in family dynamics and personal growth, was the keynote speaker (I'll say more about her presentation later).

As I discovered while floating on the lake, making

angels in the snow, and diving into piles of leaves, nature is my god. Recently, I was driving to the Orlando airport, heading into the most beautiful sunset I have ever seen. The sky was so clear, and the sun was a huge, bright ball, the perfect combination of orange, red, and yellow. I was mesmerized by the sheer size of it. Sitting precisely at eye level, I was overtaken by its beauty and felt such stillness, such reverence for nature and the universe—the same presence and stillness I experienced so many years ago at my aunt and uncle's lake house. It resurrected that innate knowing that I am connected to the same energy that makes the sun, the lake, the snow, the leaves, all of nature. At my essence, I AM part of the Source that created everything, including the sunset, and as a result, I felt the same level of reverence for myself that I felt toward the sunset. Tears rolled down my cheeks, because for the first time in a very long time, I felt completely whole. This was only possible because I'd healed a tremendous amount of pain and trauma to get to the place where I'd returned "home" to my true self.

DREDGING UP MY PAST

I'm guessing that you, too, wish to return home to your true self. That's why you picked up this book. So allow me to take you through the process that worked for me, beginning with a practice I refer to as dredging.

I grew up in Upstate New York, where the Hudson River was dredged of years of silt between 2009 and

2015. Over two and a half million cubic yards of contaminants were dredged. This silt was laced with toxic contaminants such as dioxins, PCBs, and PFAs that had been dumped higher up the river. I liken it to the emotional sludge that, during our childhood years, clogs up our own (metaphorical) inner river. In humans, the toxic elements consist of the ways we have learned to judge ourselves, criticize ourselves, put ourselves down, and limit what we can achieve.

To the degree that the sludge is toxic, our whole inner ecology becomes toxic, which is later reflected in how we relate to those we seek to connect with.

Not only did the Hudson need to be dredged over the course of many years, but the longest river in North America, the Mississippi, actually requires *ongoing* dredging. What gets dumped into the river by cities hundreds, even thousands, of miles away ruins the life-giving nature of the river, eventually creating vast acreages of a dead zone in the Gulf of Mexico.

Few of us escape an upbringing that, to varying degrees, results in an inner dead zone within ourselves. And this dead zone affects the way we see ourselves and move through the world more than most of us realize.

Because the flow of my own inner river was contaminated and the water was murky, I wasn't able to see myself as I truly am, nor could I see others as they truly are. In order to live a fulfilling life filled with peace, joy, abundance, and meaningful relationships, I learned that I needed to have a reckoning and commit to the dredging of my inner self. It was one of the greatest realizations of my life.

I wrote this book to share with you my journey to freedom from all that kept me imprisoned in a painful past so you can enjoy the same liberation I now experience on an everyday basis. To help you journey back to *your* true self, I'll take you through what I refer to as my POWER Pathway. The components of this pathway are gaining awareness of our Patterns, taking Ownership for creating the change we desire through a Willingness to heal our childhood pain, Embracing the parts of ourselves that we ignore or dislike, and finally, taking Radical Responsibility to create the life we desire.

The first part of the journey is becoming *aware* that your life is based on patterns that betray who you really are—patterns that end up masking your true self. This happens to *all* of us, so it's a fitting place to start.

PART I

PATTERNS

1

How Did I Get Here?

When people are feeling miserable—anxious, depressed, lonely, and that things aren't working out the way they hoped—they sometimes conclude that it's simply who they are. They think that it's their innate personality. They tell themselves (and others), "I've been like this all my life."

But guess what? It "isn't" just "who you are." Each of us who feels disconnected from self is likely stuck in a cycle of patterns, which consist of our belief systems and coping strategies. We develop patterns as a way to deal with life and our relationships. Such patterns might include controlling and fixing, avoiding conflict and confrontation, or overachieving as well as overcompensating, among many others. To identify those patterns (and then disrupt them), we need to first understand the concept of masks.

WHERE DOES THE PROBLEM BEGIN?

Studies demonstrate that, from day one, we mimic those closest to us. A baby who has never seen its own face will open its mouth if its caregiver opens their mouth, even sticking its tongue out to mimic a caregiver's actions.

Until quite recently (in the grand scheme of time), we had to guess at how a baby's brain works. Today we can scan a child's brain to observe what's going on inside their head in real time. We can watch how the brain's one hundred billion neurons connect with each other every second, eventually forming pathways that turn into thoughts, feelings, and emotions.

Even before birth, our brains are increasingly active, soaking up the vibes from our environment. Once we enter the world, our experiences also play a role in shaping our brains.

Around age three, the brain kicks into "use it or lose it" mode, and during the first five years, it grows faster than it ever will. It's during the first three years when the foundation for all that follows is solidified, with everyday interactions playing a key role in how we each develop. Therefore, when a dysfunctional home environment isn't addressed, a child's development can become severely limited. Studies show that the earlier we invest in a child's wellbeing, the greater the payoff.

In the world, as it's presently structured, it's not always easy for children to become the unique individuals they were born to be. To the degree that their experiences disrupt their brain's circuits, their quality of life deteriorates. The more entrenched patterns become as a result of early experiences, the more difficult it is to mitigate dysfunctional behavior.

Today we have many, many examples of the ways early adversity leads to negative outcomes. Many of us have difficulty concentrating and getting along with others, combined with an inability to control our emotions. A biological problem morphs into behavioral issues.

When a baby cries out for attention, it's vital they receive a response that affirms their inner self. When an adult responds positively, it turns off their stress response.

But what if the stress never stops? Abuse, fear, and adversity pump out toxic stress, which disrupts a child's prefrontal cortex. This is why we can't transform the lives of children without first transforming the family system.

When my kids were in their formative years, I didn't have the knowledge I have now about the importance of affirming their worth or offering positive attention when they needed it. I didn't know what I didn't know.

When my son was an infant, he was dependent on falling asleep with a bottle or his pacifier in his mouth. I was reading all the parenting books in an effort to be the "perfect" mom, and I remember reading that it was unhealthy to allow my son to fall asleep in this way. He was supposed to learn how to soothe himself at the young age of eight months.

The theory was, when he woke up in the middle of the night, we should allow him to cry it out. It was okay to go in and rub his back for a moment, but then I had to leave and let him cry. Sometimes he would cry for forty-five minutes, but rather than picking him up and coddling him to reaffirm that he was safe and secure, I abandoned him. Repeatedly.

I hate that I did this to him, but I didn't know any better. Many may disagree with this way of parenting, and my job is not to argue with them. I am simply sharing what I experienced as a young mom and have learned since.

Think of all the kids who are upset for one reason or another and forced to just "get through it" without a nurturing caregiver to soothe them. I imagine so many kids feeling sad, scared, and alone, having no one to hold them and comfort them whenever they are having big emotions. Eventually, they learn to stuff their feelings and bury their pain. This is when the masks come on, and many begin to act out.

Many teens and young adults feel unloved, disconnected from their parents, and unworthy, as if they can never do anything right, just as I did in my younger years. Because they feel an inner void and loneliness, they try to fill it with food, drugs, alcohol or anything else that might emotionally numb them. Women (who are also moms) doing the work of unmasking and healing their childhood wounds can help teach their children not to give their power away as they journey toward adulthood. By doing so, they can learn earlier than I (and many others) did that they don't have to please others all the time. They can feel confident speaking up for themselves and know that their well-being is more important than other people's expectations, opinions, and judgments of them.

We developed patterns as a strategy to cope with difficult situations as a way of protecting ourselves. We believed at one time that it wasn't safe to be who we truly were, so we covered up that person with masks. The masks are a representation of our patterns. They develop early in life as we learn to hide our true thoughts and feelings. And we likely have several of them hanging in our closets, ready to be put on at a moment's notice. Many people who feared rejection and abandonment as children began putting on masks. To be clear, we didn't have any idea we were doing this. It happened subconsciously. Anytime a moment arises when we feel it's not safe to be who we are, we put on a mask.

This is where the concept of masks transfers into one of patterns. After we've gotten comfortable wearing masks for a long enough period of time, we find ourselves living patterns, not a life.

DIMMING MY LIGHT
Allow me to go back several decades so you can

better understand who I was and how I felt before I started putting on masks to cover up my true self.

My imagination and creativity were strong before the age of ten. I knew exactly what it felt like to be my true self. I dreamed "big" all the time and had a strong belief that I was capable of doing anything.

I remember an afternoon when I was about eight years old when I set out to do a flip off the monkey bars in my backyard. It wasn't enough for me to just go across the bars one rung at a time like most kids did. I wanted to do something more daring and challenging—I wanted to *hoist* my body above them. It was a struggle to pull my body weight up enough to poke my legs through the bars, straddle the sides, and pull myself through so I was sitting on top, but once I finally did, I sat there for a moment, looking down at the ground. I won't lie, I was scared and wanted to get down. But my determination to challenge myself was stronger than my fear of heights. The next step was to slowly turn over so I was lying on my stomach, perpendicular to the bars. Once I got into position, I moved myself toward the edge. Holding onto the cold metal bars, I once again nervously stared down at the ground. I looked around to see if anyone was watching, and realizing I was alone, I feared that if I fell and got hurt, no one was around to help. After a few moments, I propelled my body forward, let go of the bars and flipped until I landed on my feet. As I realized I pushed through my fears and accomplished what I set out to do, I suddenly felt like I had superpowers.

This feeling—that I was capable of doing anything—led to the belief that I could be a professional ice skater, a gymnast, a singer, or a dancer. I was good at ice skating, I could do cartwheels and "roundoffs," and I loved to sing and dance in my kitchen, putting on performances for my mom. She thought I was great, and so did I. Being on stage in front of large audiences was something I dreamed of doing, a dream I still harbor today.

When playing on the monkey bars and dancing in my bedroom, I felt like I could take over the world, but while at school, I was still figuring out who I was around other people. It was completely opposite the way I felt when I was by myself in the backyard, in nature. I was a good kid, and teachers always commented that I was a pleasure to have in class because I wasn't disruptive. But the truth was, I was quiet because I was afraid to be my true self out loud. I was already conditioned by this point to be a "good" girl. Not to mention, I grew up in an era when kids were supposed to be seen not heard. I witnessed classmates who disrupted class, got into trouble and I certainly didn't want that to be me. I wanted to be seen and appreciated as my true self. I wanted to feel like I mattered.

For the most part, my inner light shined brightly back then. Until one day, I tried out for the lead in "Snow White." I was turned down because I couldn't sing, or so I was told. I was again turned down in middle school when I tried out for the lead role in "Grease."

Later, in high school, I wanted to play forward on the soccer team. After all, the forward is the one who gets to score. They're the one who's seen. Instead, the coaches only let me play defense. The way that I collectively interpreted these events was, "Who am I to shine my light brightly enough to be in a lead role?"

Being rejected from lead roles caused me to start playing smaller. I stopped trying to put myself out into the world. The reason I started playing smaller was because it was safer. If I didn't challenge myself the way I had on the monkey bars, I wouldn't have to face the possibility of being rejected or told that I wasn't good enough. That feeling of not being good enough caused me to feel immense shame, that there was something wrong with me or bad about me.

An inner war was going on inside me—on one hand, I wanted to shine my light, but on the other hand, I was too afraid. I told myself, "Let me be Snow White. I can sing and dance." Then I argued back, "No you can't. Play smaller. You're safe there." When I was being my true self (doing flips off the monkey bars, thinking I was superwoman), I didn't feel seen, heard, or validated in a way that resonated, but when I put myself out there, I was rejected.

All this might seem perfectly normal for a young kid. Many kids get turned down for things. But I took it personally and was devastated, believing it meant I wasn't good enough. My teachers and coaches encouraged me to dive into supporting roles, working on the props or playing defense, but the deep sense of rejection I felt when I wasn't picked for a lead role lingered.

Around the same time I was rejected to be Snow White, a teacher by the name of Mr. Parillo entered the picture. A balm to the wound I felt after not getting these leading roles, he informed my parents that I was capable of applying myself more. For some reason, I was at this meeting, and when I heard my teacher say I was capable of more, it triggered something in me that wanted to please him. So I worked harder.

As I started receiving positive feedback from Mr. Parillo on my papers, it created endorphin hits that caused me to seek further validation. That was when I started wearing the masks of performing, perfecting, and pleasing in order to get the external validation that made me feel like I was "enough." That made me feel seen. That made me feel connected.

Although I still knew what it felt like to be my true self—and felt it any time I was in nature or playing by myself—I suspect that the wound of not feeling that I was worthy existed before I was rejected for that first lead role, Snow White.

I lived in an emotional climate throughout my childhood, especially from birth to age six, that had a deep and lasting effect on me. While it serves no one to recall specific events in detail, I'm well aware of the patterns that became entrenched in me as a result.

This household dynamic was a secondary contributor to my starting to wear masks and show up the way I thought others needed me to show up. I also learned well how to be codependent, and living in such an environment contributed to my becoming hyper-vigilant.

I also remember times when I was a little girl and my mom would get upset with me or yell at me for what felt like an inconsequential reason, the tiniest of infractions. During these moments, I would curl up on the floor in a fetal position between my bed and the wall where there was just enough space to wedge my tiny body and sob. I don't know if my mom knew I was so upset, but she never came to console me. To be clear, it wasn't my mom's fault that she didn't nurture me in the way that I needed. I was too young to understand it myself. I certainly was not privy to the emotional pain and trauma that my mom endured, pain that prevented her from being attuned to what I needed. Many parents of that generation were not attuned to what their children needed, and honestly, for a long time I wasn't attuned to my children's needs either. It was a generational pattern that, without recognition, I would perpetuate.

Nonetheless, feeling like I'd been left alone was such a painful feeling for me. What I concluded was that my needs were not important, and no one was available to help me work through my feelings.

NAVIGATING PUBERTY

As luck would have it, I approached puberty in seventh grade. I was one of the first in my class to hit this critical stage in a girl's life. Prior to this, I gravitated toward playing with girls. I was thin and didn't pay much attention to my body. I liked wearing cute clothes, and it was easy to find options that fit me well. Then everything changed, seemingly overnight.

My thighs, boobs, and hips rapidly expanded. In fact, I still have stretch marks from the speed at which they grew. In the locker room, I hated getting undressed in front of my peers. I felt so self-conscious, especially on days when we had swim class. I had a hard time finding bathing suits that gave me sufficient support and had to wear Playtex bras that made me feel like a grandmother. They were the only ones that fit.

I started to feel different from most other girls. I saw myself as overweight and grew to loathe the way my body looked, often comparing my body to those of my best friends, who I saw as pretty and thin. In gym class, even with those full-coverage, grandmotherly Playtex bras, my boobs bounced everywhere. It didn't help when the boys teased me, calling me Hooters or Thunder Thighs. I felt embarrassed and powerless because I couldn't control what was happening to my body.

When I was twelve or thirteen, I visited a diet center with my mom and two friends. I asked my mom to take me because I was sick and tired of the boys making fun of me. In addition, I hated how I looked, and I was tired of my clothes feeling too tight and was desperate to change my body. My mom had always struggled with her weight, so when I asked if we could go, she thought she would try to lose weight too. While I was the one who suggested the visit, I hated being at the diet center because being there made me feel bad about myself, but not doing anything about my weight made me feel miserable as well. I felt powerless and hopeless not being able to control the outcome while also clueless that managing my weight and being at war with my body would become a life-long battle.

On this occasion, I wore a black leotard with white tights. The walls were full of mirrors, reflecting my image. If I didn't already feel ashamed as I saw myself in those mirrors, the exercise machine they had me get on definitely did the trick. The band that wrapped around my waist jiggled my fat, and as I watched my body in the mirror, bouncing and shaking everywhere, I just wanted to cry.

I had started to believe that feeling included and connected to others was also dependent on my clothing size and the number on the scale, and so began a long battle of binge/restrict eating. I would go through long periods of restricting my food intake to lose weight, and during those periods I felt good about myself. Eventually, the restrict part of the cycle was followed by a long period of binging and overeating. It was a never-ending cycle.

I wished I had someone who would have comforted me and reminded me that I was worthy, no matter what. That who I was *under* whatever extra weight I may have been carrying was more than enough to attract and keep good friends. I longed to have my mother hold me, nurture me, and tell me I mattered.

In eighth grade, when I started to be interested in boys, it seemed that none of them saw me, which only exacerbated the feelings of rejection I had from the "Snow White" episode. Boys I liked didn't like me, and I felt certain it was because of the way I looked. From eighth until eleventh grade, I believed boys were only interested in me because I had large breasts.

When I was in middle school, I loved playing football and was quite good at it, so the boys often invited me to play with them. I suspected, however, that the only reason I was invited was so the boys could pass me the ball and tackle me. At times I found myself underneath six boys, all trying to get a feel of my boobs while I gasped for air.

Because I was so desperate to feel that I belonged, coupled with the fact that I was unable to assert myself and stand up to these boys, I continued to show up again and again, hoping for a different outcome. But the outcome was always the same. I allowed the boys to tackle me, and I hated it so much that I just froze. To cope, I disassociated from my body, telling myself it was "no big deal."

The pain of longing to belong led me to become sexually active at a young age. I wanted more than anything to be accepted, and if a guy showed interest in me, it meant that I was finally being seen. It didn't occur to me that I should save my body and spirit for someone special. My survival instinct to fit in overrode any rational decision to wait for a guy who genuinely cared about me and not just my body. The choices I made, allowing myself to be a "piece of meat," only magnified my feelings of disconnection and unworthiness. It didn't make sense: On the outside, I was popular, smart, athletic, and outgoing but not good enough to be someone's girlfriend.

It's important to note that at the time that all of these pivotal events were happening, I had no idea they would serve as the blueprint for how I would put on masks for years to come rather than be my true self.

Many of us feel or have felt like we aren't pretty enough, thin enough, rich enough, strong enough, or smart enough. So much so that when another *does* show interest in us, we get a false sense of worthiness and connection. Often, these relationships aren't good for us, but we are too blind to realize it and allow mistreatment, accepting breadcrumbs from others.

THE ACCOLADES CONTINUE

Because I was suffering from a perpetual case of unworthy-itis, I doubled down on my efforts to perform, perfect, and please. Constantly performing and receiving external validation distracted me from the deep pain I was carrying.

In eighth grade, I received so many accolades I practically floated through the school's hallways. I became president of the student council and gave a speech on graduation night. I also received an award for being an outstanding student.

The road didn't stop there. I eventually fell into the "lead role" I'd always coveted. I went on to become captain of the softball team, joined the marching band, got elected into the National Honor Society, and was named president of the junior class. I became a starter on the soccer team and played for four years. I was also into horseback riding and a sought-after babysitter.

The problem was, I was wearing masks in each of these roles. My overall intentions had changed. Back when I was ten, when I genuinely believed I would make a great Snow White, I was being my truest self. But in high school, I only wanted to be seen in order to know that I was enough. For god's sake, I played the flute, but I couldn't play and march at the same time! By all reasonable standards, I was excelling, but none of it was authentic.

To boot, even though I was excelling, I *still* had people telling me I wasn't good enough. When applying to colleges, my guidance counselor told me not to apply to one particular school because it would be too difficult for me to get in. He said my SAT scores were too low, and I didn't have a resume that would be impressive enough for that type of school. Again, I heard, "Don't shine your light. Play smaller." The irony? I did apply, and I was accepted! Even though I felt defeated when my guidance counselor told me I wasn't good enough to get in, I had enough confidence from all the accolades I'd become used to receiving to apply.

The pattern of playing small and dimming my light continued into adulthood. When my son was born, I became a stay-at-home mom, nurturing my first child while supporting my husband's career. While he grew and shined brighter each year, I fell into the background and lost myself in the roles of mom and wife. My dreams fell by the wayside. The childlike wonder and awe combined with a belief that I could do anything had disappeared. What happened to the girl whose reflection used to stare back at me from the still water at my aunt and uncle's lake house?

I had become someone who was living out patterns, not a life.

2

Living Out Patterns

Eventually, the behaviors we've adopted to protect ourselves become patterns, a combination of thoughts, beliefs and behaviors that we've been carrying out for a long time. And before we know it, we are living out our patterns, not our life.

It may *feel* like our life because it feels familiar, but the sad truth is, we're only playing out our patterns. If we don't become aware of these patterns, we'll continue to live them out (by wearing masks), and others won't have the opportunity to see and love us for who we innately are. We can't change what we are unaware of, which is why it's important to understand how these patterns come about and what it looks like when we show up wearing a mask.

I once heard a story about an ancient statue that appeared to be composed of plaster and clay. After surviving severe weathering during a drought some years prior, the plaster had begun to crack.

While peering at the statue, a group with flashlights noticed something strange through one of the cracks. What stared back at them appeared to be gold, and when officials removed the plaster, the statue turned out to indeed be made of pure gold. It had been plastered over to help it survive difficult times.

This story deeply resonated with me, as I imagine it will with many others. So many of us are like this statue. We have a gold interior, but experiences in our childhoods covered it with plaster, masking our true nature. Thus, we began to live out patterns while wearing our masks.

As we move toward adulthood, life begins the difficult task of chipping away at this plaster if we allow it to, cracking us open so that we can discover the gold within. As we chip away, we gradually unhook from our patterns, allowing our gold to shine.

FEAR OF VULNERABILITY

One of my deeply ingrained patterns was avoiding vulnerability. I was petrified to be vulnerable because I feared being rejected or told I was wrong or bad for how I felt.

Thinking back, I've always been an introspective person who longed to connect with others by having heart-to-heart conversations. This is how I yearned to connect with those closest to me, but the reality was that, when I was a young child, my loved ones didn't connect on that level. I remember making attempts to share my beliefs, thoughts, or feelings, only to have the other dismiss me. It stung every time, so I kept things on a surface level where I felt safer. We discussed the weather a lot! I wanted to feel connected to those around me but didn't know how. Rather than being true to myself, I put on masks that enabled me to feel comfortable staying at surface level.

Closeness isn't the same as intimacy. Intimacy involves the risk of letting others see who we are behind our masks. It requires a level of vulnerability. If someone doesn't like what we reveal, the result might be a lack of closeness. But what many of us call "closeness" isn't actual closeness; it's a pseudo-closeness. We develop a pretense that we are close to someone, but this pretense can be blown apart in a moment.

How can we feel truly close to others if we're afraid to share personal aspects of ourselves? I was too afraid to let others see the real me behind my masks. But it was like trying to put a square peg in a round hole—trying to connect in a real and vulnerable way while wearing my masks simply didn't work.

In fact, some important details of my life I kept completely secret, because I wanted to avoid being judged by those closest to me. I love rap music, but I hid this fact from certain friends, because I feared that I would be judged for listening to vulgar "thug crap." Listening to rap music didn't align with my perfectionist mask.

PERMISSION TO BE VULNERABLE

If we want to live a fulfilling life with meaningful relationships, we have to be willing to unhook from our patterns, remove our masks, and show up vulnerably with others. Brené Brown speaks of vulnerability as taking a risk to expose ourselves emotionally. She also says that when we experience shame and keep it in the closet, it's like being in a petri dish in the dark.

Vulnerability is the cornerstone of connection. We are unable to feel close to our family and friends if we don't show them who we are. Whenever I was around family and friends, I was afraid to speak up and say what I truly thought and felt. I grew up keeping silent on issues that might cause tension or conflict. In doing so, I found myself drifting into the background as others carried the conversation.

In those days, I felt invisible and completely lonely. I could easily be at a party with dozens of people around me and still feel lonely. Whenever I was chatting with others, I would put the focus on them rather than myself, asking lots of questions to keep them talking just so I didn't have to share myself with them. While my masks might have conveyed otherwise, I was so uncomfortable having the focus on myself, which is a common characteristic for a people-pleaser.

I harbored a longing to speak freely without feeling guilt for what I might say. And without sharing what I was truly feeling or thinking, I felt disconnected, separate, alone. To banish these feelings, I'd react emotionally or numb myself by overeating, staying busy, blaming and judging, gossiping, shopping, or spending too much time on my computer or phone.

"The greatest gift we can bring to any relationship is to be ourselves," says Melody Beattie, author of *The Language of Letting Go.* "We might think that others won't like us. We might be afraid that if we relax and be ourselves that the other will shame us or go away. We might worry about what the other will think. But if we relax and accept ourselves, people often feel better being around us than when we are rigid and repressed."

If others don't appreciate us, do we really want them around? Do we need to let the opinions of others control us and our behavior? Our opinion of ourselves is truly the only thing that matters, and giving ourselves permission to be who we are can have a healing influence on our relationships. A while back, I went to a psychic and believed strongly in what she shared with me. I wanted to share what I learned with my husband, but when I shared it with him, he made fun of me because it wasn't something he believed in. This stung, and it triggered a childhood wound from the times when my mom would say, "How dare you say that?" or "What is wrong with you?" This is what led me to create the belief that it wasn't safe to have my own thoughts or feelings. If you burn your hand enough by touching a hot stove, after a while you will learn not to touch it. I learned that if I didn't want to get burned, I needed to stop sharing myself with others. This sort of thing happened often, with many people in my life, so I always read the temperature of the room before deciding whether to share what was truly in my heart.

I remember how nervous I was when I first started the "Masks Off for People-Pleasers & Perfectionists" podcast. My intention was to show up as my true self, each week sharing more of myself. I was apprehensive in the beginning, because I didn't want those who knew me to find out who I was behind my masks.

Even though it has been four years since starting the podcast, I remember how nervous I felt when the first episode was published like it was yesterday. I instantly felt nauseous because it was not customary for me to share myself so vulnerably. I imagined that I would get text messages or phone calls from family members or friends letting me know that in some way they didn't approve of what I shared.

However, my soul was calling louder than my fears to forge ahead; it was finally time to start being my true self. Being vulnerable gives me an opportunity to shed even more of my masks, exposing who I really am.

The Masks We Wear

Fitting in is what we *think* we need to do in order to feel like we belong, like we're worthy, so we put on masks. As adults, we can find ourselves wearing any number of masks, depending on the particular patterns we developed in childhood. In short, any time we're living out patterns, we're wearing a mask.

The two prominent masks I wore were those of people-pleaser and perfectionist, but I also wore the caretaker, rescuer, and fixer masks.

Every one of us wears a mask on occasion to protect ourselves, to camouflage how we truly feel. But when we don't show up fully, we can't connect in the deep way we desire. When we try to maintain a semblance of selfhood by backing away from conflict, keeping our distance, or, at times, retreating into our shell, any meaningful connection we have with others evaporates. As the poet, writer, and historian Bill Copeland observed, "The same fence that shuts others out shuts you in."

I grew up terrified of being shut out, so I over-performed, even as an adult. There was a time when I bought gifts for twenty-seven people and wrapped anywhere between eighty and a hundred gifts for the Christmas holiday. One season many years ago, I sat in my basement late one December night after the kids went to bed, wrapping their gifts so they wouldn't see what I'd bought. My back ached from bending over, and I was freezing because the basement didn't have heat. I stayed up too late and was exhausted the next day. In addition, I stood in long lines to ensure that I could secure specific gifts that the kids asked Santa for; I feared that if I didn't get there early enough, they would be sold out. For the most part, I enjoyed buying gifts for my children, but there was a fine line between buying them a few gifts because I wanted to and buying way too many gifts because I wanted to be perceived as a "good mommy."

I also sent out forty or fifty Christmas cards, dressed three trees, decorated almost every inch of my house, baked tons of cookies—you get the picture. I feel exhausted even as I write this. How did I manage all that?

Standing on my feet for long hours baking was particularly difficult because of my Sjogren's diagnosis. I had a lot of joint and back pain in those days, and standing for long hours was painful. The pain, however, was not enough to stop my need to please and to be perfect.

I share this because I didn't really want to do all those things. I also didn't want to feel so stressed out that I wasn't able to enjoy the holidays. Honestly, I would've enjoyed a simple holiday where we gave gifts to the kids but not the adults.

I eventually got smart and started ordering Christmas dinner and buying all the desserts and cookies. No one cared that the food wasn't home-cooked. In fact, they preferred the restaurant food! I put so much pressure on myself to have everything be perfect, to please everyone with just the right gifts so I could be approved of and feel that I belonged. I was essentially people-pleasing, on steroids.

There are many ways that the people-pleasing mask shows up. Here are six of the most common.

An Inability to Say No

For many of us, the most difficult word to say is one of the shortest and easiest, and that word is no. Go ahead, say it out loud. The reason it's hard to say is, we're afraid people won't like us if we deny their requests (and then have to deal with our guilt over disappointing them).

We may believe that a "good" employee, child, parent, spouse, or friend never says no. When I was growing up, my mom always reminded us that Jesus put others ahead of himself. This conditioned me to believe that I was being selfish by saying no. But every time I said yes when I really wanted to say no, I felt crappy on the inside. Subconsciously, I knew I was betraying myself, and that caused me to suffer from anxiety, depression, and poor self-worth.

Because I was tired of feeling so crappy on the inside, I decided that I was going to take a stand and assert myself by saying no to something that would potentially upset others. When my kids were much younger, I finally decided that I was no longer going to be a practicing Catholic. This was a huge deal because my kids went to Catholic school and there was a strong expectation from my husband that the kids would continue to be raised in the Catholic tradition.

I had so much angst over this decision. For the longest time, I knew in my heart that it wasn't where I belonged, but I knew both my husband and mom would be upset if I stopped going and didn't force the kids to go as well. Every Sunday, I sat in church, stewing. I didn't want to be there. I wanted to take a stand and say that I was no longer going to be a practicing Catholic.

As expected, when I mentioned to my husband that I was considering leaving the church, he was upset with me. It's incredibly difficult for a people-pleaser to have anyone be upset with them, which is what keeps the people-pleaser from asserting herself. But as difficult as it was for me to declare that I was no longer going to attend church, it felt great once I made the decision. It took a lot of internal coaching to be able to follow through on this decision, but I'm so happy I did. It was an act of standing up for myself and staying true to what I believed was best for me. I still had a long road ahead before I could finally claim freedom from the guilt I once felt when saying no to others, especially my mom or husband, but this one step represented a huge victory.

Any time someone asks you to do something *for them*, take a moment to evaluate your feelings. Perhaps you don't mind helping them in that instance. If this person is always asking you to do things for them, however, especially without reciprocating, that's a different story. Maybe it's a family member or a boss who takes advantage of you because, energetically, they know you will almost always say yes.

Begin to identify what it feels like in your body when you say yes over and over, knowing deep down that you really want to say no. Why do you think you struggle so much to say no to any specific person? Are you afraid you will be rejected, yelled at, manipulated, or ostracized?

Another area where women tend to people-please by saying yes when they'd rather say no is that of sexual intimacy. When my husband and I were first together, I deeply enjoyed sex. Over time, however, things began to change. After having two kids, my body had changed tremendously, and I was too ashamed and self-conscious to want to be intimate with him. My unhealed wounds from going through puberty were resurfacing, which contributed to how horrible I felt about myself. Additionally, when I started experiencing the symptoms that would soon lead to my Sjogren's diagnosis, the last thing I felt like doing was having sex.

Any time I suspected that my husband was initiating sex, my body would freeze up, because I knew I was going to engage when I really didn't want to. I would make all sorts of excuses—I had a headache or felt bloated from overeating. The truth was, more often than not I just didn't want to be naked in front of him. I was ashamed of my body, even though I knew he never viewed me that way. As a matter of fact, I mostly wore oversized flannel pajamas to bed in an effort to be unattractive. They were a signal that read: "I am not interested in being intimate."

The problem was, I'd been conditioned to believe that it's a woman's duty to have sex with her husband. That, combined with the way I was treated by boys in my younger school years and the guilt and pressure to be a "good" wife, had a huge impact on me.

The people-pleasing part of myself told me I had to say yes, even when, in order to be true to myself, I ought to have said no. Every time I betrayed myself by saying yes, it felt like a piece of me was dying. The message I sent to myself was that it was more important to honor another person's needs than my own, and I felt like less of a person each time I acquiesced.

It can sometimes be difficult to know how to overcome the pain that comes from saying yes all the time. This is especially true when we are so busy that we don't take time to pause and notice what's really going on within us. It can also be hard to know when it's appropriate to say no when that's what we truly want to say. But when we learn to say no, we stop lying to ourselves. We learn to trust ourselves. In turn, others feel that trust emanating from us, and they realize *they* can trust us more.

Living According to Others' Expectations

"The person who was right was okay; the person who was wrong was shamed. All value and worth may have depended on being right; to be wrong meant annihilation of self and self-esteem."
–*Melody Beattie*

As a young child, I was taught that God was separate from me, the ultimate authority to whom I must bow and obey. Doing "right" was defined as doing good for others and meeting the expectations of others, whereas being "bad" meant not putting others' needs ahead of my own.

The ultimate testament to this in my own life occurred when I gave up my teaching career to start a family when I didn't even know for sure whether I wanted to have children. It never occurred to me when I started teaching that I would leave my career after six years to raise a family. In my mind, I was going to teach until I retired at fifty-five. In addition, my husband and I never had conversations prior to starting a family about me being a stay-at-home mom. I never even told him before we got married that I might not want kids. The truth is, I hadn't ever pictured myself as a mom, but because I was accustomed to making decisions based on what others expected of me, I got pregnant.

I had difficult pregnancies with both of my kids. One might argue that life was teaching me, even then, that there was a cost to ignoring my inner knowing and instead blindly following what others wanted of me.

I was thirty years old when I had my first child. I remember hearing from others that my "biological clock" was ticking and I ought to get going with having kids, because if I waited much longer, that window of opportunity would surely pass. It was this mental chatter from others, along with my husband's desire to start a family, that compelled me to go off the pill. I was terrified of getting pregnant because of all the horror stories I heard about complicated deliveries. But I did it anyway, and then, ironically or not, hemorrhaged when I had my son. Just to be clear, I was not coerced into making this decision. The point I'm trying to make isn't whether to have kids or not, it's that I made monumental decisions like this based solely on what I believed others expected from me.

Starting a family wasn't the only unchecked decision I'd made throughout my life. I followed the proverbial path of graduating from high school, going to college, having a career, getting married, having two kids, living in the suburbs, and having a fancy house—all without checking in with myself to see if these decisions were what I truly wanted. I just followed the herd, because that is what I was conditioned to do.

Because of my need to please and meet the expectations of my husband, my mom, and society at large, combined with the fact that, at those points, I hadn't taken the time to carefully assess what *I* truly wanted, I gave up teaching to start a family. Had I not followed the expectations placed on me, I feared that I would be wrong for not obeying the "rules" of life, and further, I would be deemed a "bad" girl for not following those rules. I couldn't tolerate knowing that someone would be mad at me or disapprove of me, so I remained a "good girl" and did what was expected.

Every time I abandoned myself to please someone else, I experienced trauma. We may think of trauma only in terms of being in a car accident, being assaulted, or going to war. According to Dr. Gabor Maté, a renowned speaker, bestselling author, and leading researcher on addiction, "Trauma is an invisible force that shapes our lives. It shapes the way we live, the way we love and the way we make sense of the world. It is the root of our deepest wounds." Maté states one of the ways that trauma occurs is when we abandon ourselves to remain attached to our caregiver. It's no wonder that, over the years, I developed so many strategies to numb my pain and got so comfortable wearing masks.

In hindsight, had I not given up teaching to be a stay-at-home mom, I might not have become the person I have evolved into. So, I don't regret for one second being able to stay home and raise my kids. It was through this opportunity that I was granted the time and resources to work on my personal growth.

I invite you to take time to inventory where in your life you have made a life-altering decision to meet the expectations of others. Identifying this pattern and recognizing where you are living your life for others can help you to shift out of this pattern.

Fear of Disappointing Others

Because patterns can be handed down from one generation to the next, it's no surprise that I inherited some of my mom's. One such pattern was fear of disappointing others. While my mom was not afraid to speak her mind with me, she was a people-pleaser with others, and therefore did not want to disappoint. Although I felt traumatized (even though I didn't initially know that's what I was feeling) every time I made a choice to do something I didn't want to do just to please another, I carried the torch, putting pressure on my loved ones to do what I wished for them to do. I even resorted to, dare I say, placing guilt on my kids.

One such example occurred when my kids were teenagers. I tried to pressure them into spending time with their grandmother because I knew how much my mom loved spending time with her grandchildren and didn't want to disappoint her.

My mother loved to play games, and when my kids were little, she loved to get on the floor and play with them. She loved taking them to the park, after which they'd go for ice cream. But as my kids got older and wanted to be with their friends, they weren't as interested in playing with Grandma.

I knew my mom was disappointed, because she behaved the same way when I wanted to spend time with my friends in my younger years. Being that I was still entrenched in a people-pleasing pattern and couldn't disappoint my mom, I would bribe or pressure my kids to spend time with her. I feared disappointing her, because I didn't want to feel the guilt that *I* felt as a little girl each time she was upset with me. Bribing my kids backfired. They resisted being forced into doing something that wasn't what they truly wanted to be doing. In the end, it created a disconnection between them and my mom, which was the exact opposite of what I was trying to create. My kids may have spent time with their grandma out of obligation, but I am sure my mom could feel on some level that they really wanted to be with their friends, not her.

There have been countless times throughout my

life when I've done things for or with others because I didn't want to disappoint them. I've already recounted the Christmas wrapping marathons! Feeling that others were disappointed in me was like hearing fingernails scratching a chalkboard. I learned at an early age that if I didn't do what my mom expected of me, she'd be displeased with me. As a result, she would withdraw her love until she was done being angry. I couldn't tolerate the discomfort of feeling that someone could withdraw their love at any given time. What I came to understand is that my fear of being abandoned was at the core of this pattern.

When we consistently cajole someone into meeting our needs, it becomes less likely that their honest, compassionate center will emerge. If someone wants to gratify our wishes, they will do so, if and when they are ready. We can facilitate the process and increase the likelihood of a positive response by making our wishes known, then truly letting the issue go. If there's the least amount of pressure, the other will smell it, and whenever someone makes a decision, in order for it to be true to *them*, it needs to come from their heart and not their emotions, which are often laced with volatility. Pressuring someone to do what we want them to do generates resistance, and even though a desire may technically be met, the person meeting that desire often ends up miffed.

Conflict Avoidance

One afternoon when I was eight years old, I sat on our back staircase crying and pleading with my mom to stop screaming at my cousins, who were teenagers at the time. I don't recall what she was mad at them for, but I vividly remember how out of control my mom's emotions were. After witnessing her lose control over herself countless times, I became afraid of conflict. I didn't want to ever experience the level of powerlessness I saw in her in those moments.

As a sensitive child, I felt everything my cousins were feeling, and I wanted to save them from the pain I imagined they felt as a result of my mother raging at them, even though they were much older than I was.

It's perhaps important to note that we lived in a two-family household. My grandmother and three of my cousins lived downstairs, and I lived upstairs with my parents and my sister. My three cousins lived with my grandmother because their mom (my mom's sister) died when they were only two, three, and four, and their dad abandoned the family soon afterward. My grandmother became their legal guardian, but my mom helped raise them.

My mom was only nineteen when her sister died. This caused a lot of trauma for my mom, and it was a big responsibility to help raise three young children at such a young age herself. In addition, my mom didn't have a close and loving relationship with her own mother, who was a pretty cold, unemotional woman.

So, between the trauma my mom had experienced in her own life and the unhealthy relationship she had with her own mother, she had a ton of unhealed pain. Most people in my parents' generation didn't face their demons by getting help. Therapy wasn't nearly as accessible or acceptable back then. It's understandable now why my mom was so reactive in those days, but as a child I was not privy to any of this information, which is why it was scary whenever she lost control of her emotions.

In that moment, I felt scared and upset for my cousins. I couldn't understand how my mom could be so mad at them. Again, I was too young to understand all the circumstances. I only knew how I interpreted it and how it felt. But it was from these types of experiences, of which there were many, that I learned to hate conflict and feel extremely anxious whenever my loved ones were upset with me or with one another. It was classic codependent behavior that resulted in the feeling that I was in a mental and emotional prison, one from which I yearned to be set free.

Caretaking At Our Own Expense

One of the toughest struggles is that of knowing ourselves to be both loved and lovable. We all want to experience that act of caring and feeling cared for. We long to experience the warmth and closeness of those around us, to give and receive affection.

As a young child, in an attempt to feel loved and to love others, I felt an overwhelming responsibility to take care of the emotional needs of others, especially my mom. I loved my mom so much and it killed me to see her upset. I would do anything to make her happy. I always sensed when she was unhappy, and starting at a young age, I felt it was my job to make her happy. She seemed happy with me whenever I excelled in school or did exactly what she wanted me to do. This pattern between us only solidified the people-pleaser in me, increasing my desire to take care of my mother as well as be everyone else's caretaker. And this need carried well into adulthood.

My aunt, the one whose lake house I visited during my childhood summers, asked me on her deathbed to take care of my uncle when she was gone. My uncle, who was eighty-nine at the time she died, did pretty well for himself. The only help he needed in the beginning involved his financial matters, but this became more overwhelming when I later had to settle his estate. People-pleasing and perfectionism often overlap, as you will see in the way I approached my uncle's care and, later, his estate.

One of the reasons this was so difficult was, there were many decisions to make, and perfectionists often struggle to make decisions for fear of choosing wrong, then getting blamed or shamed for it. The pressure to do everything "right" for my uncle and his estate, coupled with the resentment I felt for having to be the one doing it, seemed like a huge burden. I felt trapped. I wanted to pass this responsibility onto other family members but felt too guilty to do so.

I loved my uncle, and even today, I would probably make the same decision to be his caretaker. But when my aunt put pressure on me to take care of him, I didn't have the courage to say no, even if I'd wanted to. It was a knee-jerk reaction to say yes whenever *anyone* asked me to do something for them. This example was the epitome of what it looks like when you combine people-pleasing with perfectionism. The perfectionist part of me, which is uber competent, combined with the inability to say no locked me into taking care of others, even when they could and should take care of themselves. It's perfectly natural to be sensitive to what others think, feel, and need. However, that's different from the fixing, rescuing, or caretaking that's nothing more than an old, worn-out, codependent pattern. Over time, I gradually learned how to separate the times when I was enmeshed trying to take care of other people from times when I allowed them to take responsibility for themselves. I started to shift my perspective after I attended a number of Codependent Anonymous meetings (a twelve-step program for codependents). I realized that I was acting as a crutch for others when I took care of things they could be doing themselves.

I've learned that it's okay to be concerned and loving toward others, but it isn't my responsibility to take care of their emotional wellbeing. I need to listen and hear them out but not feel compelled to respond in the way they might prefer.

It took a long time for me to get to the place where I didn't feel pressure to take care of others' emotional wellbeing. Mel Robbins has a saying, "let them," which well describes how I started drawing a boundary. The meaning behind "let them" is that if others have expectations for what you should do for them, allow them to have those expectations without the need to act on them. Even if the other pouts, gets upset, or is frustrated because you no longer fall into the trap of meeting their needs, let them have their tantrum, and remain steady in your resolution to unhook from the caretaking pattern. If you still find yourself feeling like you are overly concerned with caring for another's wellbeing at your own expense, refrain from beating yourself up. It may take a while to unhook from this pattern, especially if you have been entrenched in it for many years.

Inability to Assert Needs

I grew up wary of doing things for myself, especially when it conflicted with something someone else needed from me. (You are likely picking up on the ways different masks can be layered upon one another!) As stated earlier, while it may have been unintentional, my parents didn't always meet my needs in the way I needed. I interpreted their actions to mean that I was unworthy of being nurtured and loved.

This subconscious belief that I was unworthy of having my wants and needs met along with the deeply ingrained pattern of caretaking continued through much of my life. As a consequence, I often felt resentful or unfulfilled because I never felt safe making my needs the priority. Learning to assert our needs is a healthy skill that allows us to be proactive, whereas the inability to say no because of a deep sense of guilt is reactive; it's coming from a place of lack and scarcity.

When I was diagnosed with Sjogren's disease, I had to learn to prioritize my needs. I was struggling to take care of my two young children and myself during the day while my husband was at work, and there were days when I experienced so much fatigue and pain that I couldn't get off the couch. I was sad that I wasn't the energetic, healthy mom who looked forward to playing with her kids. Instead, I hoped and prayed for the ability each day to at least take care of their basic needs.

Rather than giving away energy I didn't have and making myself even more exhausted, I decided to keep that energy in the tank for my children and husband. My first step: hire someone to clean the house, which felt wildly uncomfortable.

Was I asking for too much? I'd been taught that hiring someone to clean the house was frivolous, but on the other hand, I knew that having help would benefit my health. But because I didn't believe I was worthy of having or prioritizing my own needs, I struggled to give myself permission to hire someone to help keep the house clean. I told myself I was being lazy and should do it myself. In hindsight, I was far from lazy; I was sick. I did eventually hire someone, and although it was uncomfortable in the beginning, I pushed through that feeling because I knew I didn't have the strength and energy to clean. Knowing that I couldn't physically clean without being in pain and completely exhausted outweighed the mental chatter that told me I was undeserving of having a housecleaner.

I also felt guilty any time I dropped my kids off at the playroom at the gym. Even though exercise helped me feel better and my kids loved playing in the playroom, I felt like I was being selfish for putting myself first. But the saying "Put your oxygen mask on before assisting others" is absolutely true. If we don't prioritize and assert our needs, we won't be at our best to help others. Over time, as I healed that childhood wound and engaged in lots of therapy, I got to the place where I could slowly lean into the fact that my needs are important and worthy of being met.

When my kids were teenagers, they were involved in many activities. To call myself a chauffeur would be an understatement. There were days when I drove across town to their school at least three or four times a day. I drove my daughter to and from school rather than forcing her to take the bus, and when they were both in the ski club, I would pick them up late at night after already having driven back and forth to school several times. I was at the mercy of their needs, taking them from one place to another. I realize I could have said no to many of the requests, but my guilt wouldn't allow me to. Since I was making their needs a priority and much of my day was filled with attending to their wants and needs, I rarely took care of my own. I would manage to get in a workout and meet with friends here and there for tea, and I took some time while they were at school to do what I wanted to do, but the majority of my days were spent attending to them. I realize that, to some extent, this was my job as a stay-at-home mom. But my mentality originated from my people-pleasing pattern. I did what I did from an unhealthy place. If I wasn't feeling well, rather than resting and taking care of myself I pushed through, attending to the never-ending needs and wants of my kids.

I've since learned to better assert my needs and wants, and whenever I take a step backward, which is to be expected, I remember to be gentle with myself. Once I become aware that I'm putting others' needs ahead of my own (the signs of which include feeling unusually exhausted or irritable), I pause, take a deep breath, and remind myself that I am worthy. I recognize that it is just my pattern rearing its ugly head. My true self knows that I am worthy of living my life according to my desires. It took a long time to get where

I am today, and I have further to go to fully unhook from this long-standing pattern, but I am aware, and I can pivot from there. What about you? Do you speak up and ask others for what you want and need? Do you believe that you are worthy of having your needs met?

While the perfection mask and the people-pleasing mask often show up hand-in-hand, it's important to clarify the ways the perfection mask oftentimes shows up on its own. I'm extremely familiar with the perfection mask. I wore it often as both a young child and an adult. There are two primary ways this mask showed up for me and might also be showing up for you.

A Loud Inner Critic

Thierry Henry, who played soccer for Arsenal, opened his heart to share his innermost self with the *Guardian*, a leading British tabloid, explaining how he was trapped in depression during his career.

The forty-six-year-old former forward for the French team, which won the World Cup in 1998 with him as Arsenal's all-time highest scorer, said he had a moment early in the Coronavirus pandemic where he was "crying almost every day." He said those tears had been present but not acknowledged for a very long time. He linked them to his past and to a search for approval, having grown up with a father who was critical of his performances. I can relate to the way he felt, given that this need to please a parent was also a constant source of my own decades-long anxiety and depression.

Henry recalled an occasion when, as a teenager, he scored all of the goals in a 6-0 win, only for his father to tell him he shouldn't be happy, scolding him, "You missed that control, you missed that cross."

I felt deeply touched by his frank admission. Although my father never openly judged or criticized me and always lit up when I entered the room, that wasn't always the case with my mom. I know she loved me in the best way she knew how, but she had a side that was critical and judgmental. I no longer blame her for that, especially because I've grown to believe that it was through my interactions with her that I eventually healed and grew into the person I am today.

However, that critical voice that was once my mom's became my own. And unfortunately, I have had that same critical tone with my own kids.

I'm someone who's been consistently hard on myself for most of my life, believing that I should do everything perfectly. When I first started teaching, I expected I would be a perfect teacher on day one. When I struggled to relate to my students or couldn't teach a concept in a way that they could comprehend, I beat myself up. I never allowed myself to have a learning curve. I assumed that I should know everything immediately and be able to do it all perfectly. There were so many days when I cried all the way home from work, vowing that I wouldn't return the next day.

Not only did I expect that I *should* be able to do new things perfectly from day one, I also put a lot of pressure on myself to "do more and be more." It was imperative that my house look perfect. I had to be the perfect mom, daughter, wife, and friend. I tried so hard to be perfect at working out and managing my weight, always trying to eat healthier. I tried going gluten free, dairy free, alcohol free, and vegan. Have you ever tried to give up dairy, gluten, caffeine, sugar, alcohol, and grains all at once? I don't recommend it. My family didn't even want to be around me. I was very irritable!

It was easy for me to go into all-or-nothing thinking. If I didn't do everything perfectly, I'd give up and do none of it. Then I would beat myself up because I "failed." The issue isn't over- or under-eating, overspending or denying oneself, or overly attaching to another versus being avoidant. The issue is being able to find a middle ground, a balance. It may require that the pendulum swings back and forth for a while before it rests comfortably in the middle.

The internal pressure I put on myself was enough to make anyone go mad. I was exhausted from being at war with myself, and I wanted someone to free me from my mind and thoughts. What I didn't realize was that I wanted to be freed from the pattern of so readily and easily giving my power away.

The internal pressure led to overwhelm and a great deal of stress. My body was always in knots, and I lived with a near-constant stomachache, which very well could have been linked to the Sjogren's diagnosis I received in my mid-thirties.

If you also have a critical voice in your head that pushes and drives you, perhaps you could practice having more grace and self-compassion. Try breaking things into smaller, bite-size pieces when learning something new, and allow for mistakes. When you feel overwhelmed and stressed out, try applying the mantra "first things first" or "one step at a time." Remind yourself that you don't have to be perfect. If being gentle with yourself is not available to you, imagine a loved one or a pet being gentle and loving toward you until you can do it for yourself. This takes time, so be patient.

Strong Internal Pressure

One day a few years ago, I noticed that I was in a funk. Struggling to complete everything on my checklist, I became aware of an energy deficit that I tried to ignore. I munched my way through (literally) by eating like crazy, putting on a few pounds as a result. This only compounded my funk.

It didn't take long for me to realize that my deeper self was crying out to be nurtured, so I slowed myself down and set aside a day to be with myself. I journaled, meditated, cried, and then went to the beach. And you know what? I still accomplished most of the things I normally accomplish on an average day.

Because so much of my identity has been attached to how productive I am, slowing down can be incredibly difficult. It takes me back to an old tape that used to play in my head, telling me it isn't okay to just "be." The feeling of unrest I get when chasing after something new, as if my life isn't already enough, causes me to feel I need more and therefore have to do more. I've come to understand that this level of striving is linked to the fulfillment of an unmet need, the notion that if I want to be somebody, I have to perform, and I have to do so with perfection. In response, I become a human "doing," not a human "being."

This internal pressure originates from the conditioning to be "a good little girl" who lives up to the expectations of others and does what she's told. But there came a time when I grew tired of following the expectations set by others. I rebelled and had no desire to do anything at all. The problem was, when I did none of the things expected of me, I still didn't feel well—or, at the other extreme, I found I was bored and didn't know what to do with myself. That's what the funk reflected, at its core—the reminder that I no longer desire to be hyper-vigilant.

Whenever I felt off-center, I was quick to tell myself that I was doing something wrong instead of recognizing that that feeling was my body's way of sending me a message. I was holding onto an expectation that I should be on the metaphorical mountaintop at all times, never in the valley. Anything less meant something was wrong with me. There have been times when I've felt this way for days, sometimes weeks.

Nowadays, if I get into that "funk," it usually lasts only a couple of hours or, at times, a day. But I don't resist those feelings when they arise. I have learned that the point of life is not to stay on the mountaintop all the time.

For me, the antidote to all-or-nothing perfectionistic thinking was to cultivate a practice of living in the gray area. Rather than give up on all the things I do in a typical day, I reframed my mindset to embrace the fact that I don't have to do everything perfectly.

Do you rush through your day trying to get things done? Do you race against the clock from one task to the next? Do you enjoy a sense of accomplishment when you check off each of the many tasks on your to-do list or do you put pressure on yourself to hurry? How do you feel about yourself whenever you fail to complete what you set out to accomplish? If you're sick or exhausted, do you tell yourself to "muscle through it"?

Are you ready to examine the expectations you have for your life? If they are outdated, are you willing to cast them aside and set your spirit free? Are you, too, ready to change the story you tell yourself, the running narrative constantly playing in your head? Are you willing to focus on your patterns so you can unhook from them?

You alone can rewrite your story. Friends, coaches,

and therapists can support you, but you are the one who has to do the work. Is the work easy? No. But it's so worth it to feel worthy and lovable, free of anxiety and depression, and empowered to create the life you desire. In my case, I began to experience a previously unknown measure of peace and joy—a deep sense of abundance, even. If you are sick and tired of repeating the same old story, realize that though this pattern runs deep within you, it can be sent packing if you are willing to commit to doing the work.

Ironically, my suggesting that you "take ownership" can easily become yet another responsibility you feel you have to shoulder. Please don't fall into this trap. I changed my narrative by gradually learning to nurture myself, be gentle with myself, and immerse myself in self-compassion.

To be gentle with ourselves strikes at the root of our belief that we have to do everything perfectly. It helps us learn to trust ourselves so that we're able to tune into and follow our intuition. I'll talk more about intuition later, but for now, remember that as you learn to trust yourself more fully, others will learn that you are reliable and trustworthy, which is a critical component of the connection you seek.

PART II

OWNERSHIP

4

Growing Ourselves Up

To reach the personal freedom you seek, you'll need to take responsibility to fill the void inside yourself by healing your childhood wounds instead of counting on others to do it for you or change their ways in order to accommodate yours.

When I first met my husband, I was attracted to certain qualities that were present in him and not in me. He was strong, stable, assertive and decisive. On a subconscious level, these must have been qualities that I wanted to possess because they weren't developed in me as I grew up. I didn't realize when I was younger that I constantly drew people into my life who had strong assertive traits to help me ultimately recognize where I needed to work on myself so *I* could be strong and assertive. It's only in hindsight that I understand this.

In the beginning of our relationship, my husband

was very attentive. He planned special nights out and insisted on paying for everything. He worried about my safety. He took me shopping and helped me pick out clothes.

I felt secure about myself and believed I was happy because he validated me, often telling me I was special to him and he felt lucky to have me. He was the classic knight in shining armor! He saved me from the aching void within me, the one I'd attempted to fill with either food or performing.

This aching void, which I refer to as the "hole in the soul," was the result of repeatedly betraying my true self. Each and every time I chose to put on a mask instead of being the real me, a part of my soul was dimmed. My soul came into this world *whole*, but it developed *holes* when I abandoned my true self to stay attached to another, first and foremost, my mother.

Since no one can fill an aching void for us, it was my responsibility to heal my own childhood wounds. My husband beautifully reflected to me the areas in which I needed to grow, and I had to set him free from the burden of filling the voids within me. It took many years before I was able to see that this was an inside job, and only I could liberate myself from the mental prison I was in. I had to stop living from my child self and allow my adult self to emerge. This is how we grow ourselves up.

As the years progressed, my husband stopped behaving in the ways I'd become accustomed to. The honeymoon phase wore off and reality set in, no doubt because my patterns were resurfacing and the masks were being put on more and more often, sometimes, it seemed, with glue. And, at the same time my patterns were coming out, so were my husband's.

His patterns clashed with mine, causing much resistance and, at times, friction in our relationship. At the time, I didn't realize that I needed to experience the pain of butting up against his way of doing things in order to become stronger. I was like a caterpillar in the chrysalis, and I needed to struggle within the relationship to become the woman I am today.

Over the thirty plus years that we have been married, we've owned six houses together, and with each one, we've embarked upon multiple renovations. We've painted, bought furniture, and reconstructed entire rooms. A few years ago, we renovated our current primary bathroom. We completely gutted it and started from scratch. Up until that point, I was accustomed to allowing him to make a majority of the decisions because in the past, if I tried to assert my opinions or wishes and they clashed with his, we ended up arguing over stupid things, and I acquiesced to keep the peace.

Over time, as I became stronger in my sense of self, I determined that it was important for me to speak up at times to get the outcome I desired. I wanted a particular type of tub for one of the bathroom projects, and I didn't give up until we agreed. When a particular decision was really important to me, I stood my ground, and when a decision wasn't that big of a deal, I let it go.

When my husband and I first met, I was emotionally immature. Looking back, I recognize that I was looking for someone who could take care of me, because that's what I believed to be true love. The way I felt when I was with him in the beginning was something I'd never felt before. I never had someone adore me the way he did. But the truth is, it couldn't have been true love, because I didn't even know what true love was! I certainly didn't love myself in those days, and I was accustomed to "feeling" loved only when I was being a "good" girl. What I knew and learned growing up was *conditional* love and dependence.

Because I spent so much in my adult life seeking and searching for someone on the outside to make me feel worthy and lovable, I ended up feeling like I was in survival mode most of the time. We are biologically wired for connection; it's a universal basic and inherent need. But I didn't feel that deep sense of connection because I was in survival mode, and when we are in survival mode, what we feel is dependence.

In actuality, it was my little-girl self that was interacting with my husband most of the time. We had a weird parent-child dynamic, one wherein I constantly sought his approval and craved the safety and stability he created for the kids and me. I showed up wearing my people-pleasing and perfection masks most of the time, afraid my true self wouldn't be enough. But because I wasn't showing up *as* my true self, I felt lonely and disconnected.

I wondered, *How can I feel love when all I feel is dependence?* Real love would have looked like my whole, healed self meeting my husband's whole, healed self. From this space we would be able to see the gold within each other rather than hide behind our protective masks. But this wasn't the case, and it was difficult for me to communicate with him in a way he could relate to, and vice versa. I often felt misunderstood and unseen, and I would walk away from conversations feeling, once again, like there was something inherently wrong with me. I was in victim mode, and to get out of victim mode, I needed to take ownership and "grow myself up."

If we pay attention, those close to us—our families as well as our friends—mirror to us the roadblocks that prevent us from being true to ourselves. In doing so, they allow us to grow ourselves up if we're willing to take that step. I am deeply thankful for my husband, as the act of being willing to peer between my cracks—just as the authorities did with the plaster-covered statue of the Buddha—allowed the gold not only to be uncovered but also to feel safe staying uncovered.

RELEASING BLAME

The years when I was dependent on my husband to fill my needs created many issues in our relationship.

My sense of self had become incredibly weak, and I blamed my husband for how miserable I felt. Whenever there is a victim, there is a villain, and I made my husband that villain.

Blaming was the only way I knew to "fix" the situation. Remember, one of the masks I wore was that of "fixer." I believed that if he would only listen to me and do things the way I thought he should do them, everything would be fine. I wouldn't have to look in the mirror and change my patterns if he would simply change his. The reality is that we can't change other people, so I felt powerless.

I saw him as a judgmental, critical, and rigid villain when, in truth, *I* was judgmental, critical, and rigid with myself, constantly judging myself and feeling like I was falling short. My husband was only mirroring the way I saw myself, and I needed to break free from that in order to live the life I desired.

As I've mentioned, it took a long time for me to understand that if I wanted real change in my life, I needed to put down the torch of blaming my husband. That was difficult to do at times because many of his behaviors were simply not okay. In fact, I remember some excruciatingly painful sessions at family therapy when the things said and the feelings hurt aren't experiences I'd ever want to go through again. The car ride home from those sessions were some of the longest of my life. I believe that we needed to go through that as a family to get to where we are today, but my point is that during those sessions, I made my husband the villain and myself and the kids the victim. I didn't know any other way to relate.

What I knew for sure was that I didn't want our son and daughter to grow up in victim mode, nor did I want them to relive the eggshell environment I grew up in. My heart longed for an environment where we could all be open, honest, and real with each other. We have that environment today because I stopped waiting for my husband and kids to change and instead started focusing on myself. I plugged away at healing my past and learned how to change my mindset. These were two of the most pivotal pieces when it came to creating a life in which I can consistently show up as my whole self.

As I look back on the way I lived my life before I started removing my masks, I see how much of a victim role I played. I often griped about how this person or that person transgressed against me. It was customary to gripe about what my mom, husband, or friends "did" to offend me. Rather than standing up for myself and setting a boundary, I remained the victim because I chose to wait for *them* to change.

A huge shift started to occur when I accepted that others are not likely to change. I was the one who had to shift and grow up. It was scary at first to set boundaries and admit that I needed to be stronger and more assertive. I started taking small steps, asserting myself in less critical moments. Over time, like building a muscle, my abilities got stronger. Finally, I was able to let go of blaming others and take responsibility for being the strong, capable person I show up as today.

I CREATE MY REALITY

Life has a way of setting us up to grow—if we are willing to pay attention. I met my husband in a bar where both of us worked at the time. We were in our twenties, and it was customary for many of the workers to go out and drink after hours. We also spent a lot of time drinking with friends. The habit of centering our pleasure time around drinking continued after we married. We had many parties in our backyard or basement, and drinking was at the center of these get-togethers.

While I enjoyed myself to a degree, I knew that drinking and partying was also a way of avoiding being true to myself. I wasn't connecting with others in a way that was true to my nature. At times, I felt ashamed after partying long and hard.

Once I became a parent, the shame continued, because I often resented the weekends, perceiving myself as chained to my children's wants and needs. As the provider, my husband worked all week, and I felt pressure to be there for the family. I didn't feel that I had permission to do things for myself.

When I did take time to perhaps go out to dinner with a friend, I was extra-conscious of the time. I worried whether I was out too late. I worried whether I was being selfish and felt a nagging pull to hurry up and get home. I just wanted to be free and live my life without feeling so much guilt.

For a long time, I continued to put on my masks and pretended to be the person I thought others wanted me to be, avoiding conflict whenever possible. I simply gave in and made it comfortable for others. If I sensed that my husband was even slightly upset with the kids or me, I did all I could to please, control, fix, and manage everyone so I could feel less anxious.

I used to feel scared, frustrated, and angry every time I tried to stand up for myself, only to back down and be silent. Rather than being an adult and providing safety for the little girl inside myself, I fell apart.

One day, I started asking myself what it would take for me to feel and act like an adult. Each time I asked that question, the answer was, "Continue to work on myself by reparenting my child self so she can feel safe." I had to reassure myself that I *am* an adult, and it is perfectly normal and reasonable to live life according to my expectations, not the expectations of others.

Time and time again, I had to take the spotlight off my husband and shine it on the areas where I needed to grow. I would ask myself, "What wounds still need healing so I can show up in our relationship as an equal?"

We no longer have backyard parties like we used to. I couldn't continue to put myself through that and feel like I was betraying myself. I still like to go out to dinner with friends and enjoy a couple of drinks, but I show up more authentically.

I have come a long way since then because I've learned two things. One, I was co-creating my reality. What this means is that I had to take responsibility for the part I played in keeping myself stuck in my patterns. No one was holding a gun to my head, forcing me to do things I didn't want to do. All that time I'd spent keeping myself busy enabled me to avoid confronting reality, ameliorating the deep pain I had chained myself to. Two, if I wanted to be free, I would have to be the one to create my reality, all on my own. Somewhere deep inside myself, I realized that I was the one keeping my true self locked away. If I wanted real freedom from living out patterns and not a life, I had to recognize and take ownership of the various ways I was keeping myself imprisoned.

Confronting the Truth

Without the willingness to confront my actions over the years, I would not have been able to take responsibility for becoming a better parent. I had to realize that my unconscious behavior was stemming from my unhealed wounds, and it was my job to heal those wounds. I'm going to share some uncomfortable stories with you, not to shame myself but to show that if we want to make change in any part of our lives, we first must be willing to confront the truth, then do what is necessary to take different actions going forward.

I first realized that I needed to change my parenting patterns after I attended a conference where Dr. Shefali was the keynote speaker. It was the first time I had heard of her, but Oprah has endorsed her groundbreaking work as "revolutionary." I cried throughout her entire talk because she was speaking to my soul and to the child within me. I knew something was "off" in the way I was relating to my kids, but I couldn't identify what it was until I later read Dr. Shefali's book, *The Conscious Parent*. This book (and her work overall) changed my life.

As I began to take responsibility for how I was harming my kids, I learned to show up differently. It was only when I made a conscious decision to understand why I was behaving unconsciously that I was able to have a whole new perspective on parenting my kids. From this new perspective, I was more openhearted and able to focus on their gold rather than reacting to their behaviors, behaviors that mostly stemmed from their own unmet needs. It took a long time to be able to show up more consciously. After all, I had many layers of unconscious behavior to heal from. Hopefully the following stories illustrate how my unconscious behaviors manifested.

From the day they were born, I set out to save my kids from pain. By constantly trying to solve their problems for them rather than allowing them the opportunity to struggle like the caterpillar struggles to become a butterfly, I clipped their wings.

It was with the best of intentions that I tried to help them avoid any suffering they might be faced with. Truthfully, I was also trying to soothe the anxiety and worry I felt when I witnessed them struggle (because remember, part of me desired to save others from discomfort).

When our kids were young, I wanted to save them from ever upsetting their dad. I was the fixer, rescuer, and peacemaker. It was exhausting.

Whenever I sensed my husband might get angry or anxious about something my son or daughter was doing, I'd say, "Don't say that in front of Dad because he will get mad." My little-girl self was walking on eggshells, afraid of upsetting "Daddy." Reflecting my pattern as a little girl, which was to become anxious and have a freeze response anytime others were arguing, my body would tense up and my heart would race. I didn't want to condition my kids to live in such an environment, but at that time, my scared little self was driving the bus, and all I knew to do was stop the tension before it started.

My unconscious behavior showed up again when I made tidiness a priority with my kids, an approach that created an especially sore spot with my daughter when she was much younger. Her room was often a mess, with clothes and food wrappers everywhere. My husband and I both yelled and nagged at her about the state of her room. When she resisted and fought back, we doubled down on our anger. There was a time when I was fed up with the clutter in her closet, so I started cleaning it myself, and as I did so, I made comments about how disgusted I was. I knew she was taking it personally.

When I was a teenager, my room and closet were meticulous. Every item of clothing was color-coded and everything had its place. I had these tendencies because it was one of the only ways I felt in control when much of my life felt out of control. As a mother, I projected my own unhealthy need for neatness and orderliness onto both of our children. I was on them constantly to pick up and often made snide comments that surely caused them to feel shame.

It's critical to teach our children important life skills, but lecturing doesn't do the trick. We need to model productive ways of dealing with things. I regret that I made neatness and cleanliness a priority over their wellbeing. The truth is, having a clean and neat room is generally not important to kids. Now, at twenty-one, my daughter's apartment is neat and orderly. She half-jokingly blames us for giving her OCD tendencies!

I also recall a time with my son I'm not proud of. It happened when he was just two years old. It was dinner time, and he refused to eat his broccoli. He ate his chicken nuggets and mac and cheese but would not touch the broccoli. Because I'd read in all the books how important it was to make sure kids ate their fruits and vegetables, I told him he couldn't leave the table until he ate them. He begged and cried to get down, but I wouldn't let him leave the table.

It broke my heart to see him so upset. I was in turmoil because a part of me knew it was ridiculous to force him to eat his broccoli, but the other part of me—the part that needed to be a "good" mom—wouldn't give in. I had to go to another room so I wouldn't see how upset he was, occasionally popping my head in to ensure he was safe. It was unbearable to see him cry all alone. In hindsight, it reminded me of all the times I was left all alone, sobbing with no one consoling me. He sat there by himself for almost two hours, strapped into his booster seat, before I finally gave in and let him leave the table.

Years later when I reflected on this, I felt like such a bad mom. Who makes their kid sit strapped in his booster seat for two hours by himself while a parent forces him to eat broccoli? The truth of the matter was, I did it because I was trying to make myself feel worthy as a mom by doing all the "right things." But all I really did was shame and traumatize my son. At the time, I was unconscious and unaware of the effect my actions would have on my kids.

I had a similar experience years later when my daughter was nine. I was taking her to a ski lesson at a small mountain about forty minutes from our house. When we were about ten minutes from the mountain, she realized she forgot her ski pants. She only had on a pair of thin leggings she typically wore underneath her ski pants.

When she told me she had forgotten her pants, I saw a wave of shame and fear wash over her. She had good reason to feel this way, because I went ballistic. I screamed, yelled, and shamed her so badly that she bawled her eyes out. I shouted, "How could you do this? We were almost there, and I drove all this way for nothing. You can go home and miss your lesson or ski in your leggings and freeze."

I know what you must be thinking, and I hear you. This was not one of my prouder moments. I heard my mother's words come right through my mouth, and I was flabbergasted. How many times have I walked out the door and forgotten something because I was distracted? We have all done this at some point, and yet I expected my daughter not to make the same mistake. I was that hard on myself about many different things, never allowing myself to make mistakes, and I projected that onto her.

Afterward, I felt horrible and struggled to understand why I couldn't manage my emotions. This wasn't the type of mom I wanted to be. I could see what my words and actions had done to my young, impressionable daughter. If I had understood the gravity of my words all along, would I have been able to do better in those early years? I'm not entirely sure of the answer to that, because I had layers of my own pain that had to be healed. When my kids were young, I was only just beginning to learn how to grow myself up.

When my son was a new teenager, I was desperate to feel close and connected to him, so I put pressure on him to connect with me—just as my mother had done to me. Whenever we were in a conflict, I forced him to sit and talk about his feelings. During these discussions, I'm sure I was reactive and most likely said things that made him feel ashamed. I remember times when I discounted his feelings and talked over him. Naturally, he wouldn't want to sit with me and have a heart-to-heart when he was fuming at me! In those moments, the last thing he'd want to do is connect with me.

My intentions were good; I was trying not to sweep an issue under the rug the way we'd done in my house growing up. If I hurt my son with something I said or did, I wanted to talk about it. But the reality was, he was a thirteen-year-old boy who hadn't been taught to share his feelings. If anything, he learned from his father and me that it wasn't safe to speak up. And when he attempted to do so, he learned that it was like placing his hand on a hot stove. In the end, I made him share with me because of *my* needs, not his.

In an effort to feel close to him, there were times I felt like I had to behave in a certain way. I felt as if I were hustling for his love and approval. I came to understand that this behavior came from the belief that it wasn't enough to be myself, that if I were my whole self with my son, he wouldn't want to be around me. So I played it safe. Much of the time, I said what I thought he wanted to hear. If I said something that irritated him, I backed off because I didn't want him to pull away from me. I was afraid that if I spoke my truth, it would damage the relationship, but the fact of the matter is, not being truthful is what ruins relationships.

When I got honest with myself, I realized that it was more important to share the whole truth about myself, even if it meant he wouldn't want to be close to me. I no longer wanted to be fake and superficial. This was a big risk for me to take, because there was a chance he may not have liked it when I shared openly and honestly and might have pulled away. While it was scary at first to try on this new behavior, I knew I had to be true to myself. At the same time, I reminded myself that my son and I had the best chance of having a close and healthy relationship if I was willing to be honest and transparent about who I truly was and how I truly felt.

While I was learning to navigate my relationship with my son, I still had a ways to go with my daughter. My daughter and I have had some tumultuous times when her strong-willed self butted up against my anxious, worried self. We got into big arguments over her going to certain friends' houses or doing particular things I wasn't comfortable with. She felt I was being unreasonable and too controlling. On some level in several instances, I was allowing my fear to dictate my decisions.

When she was angry with me and said hurtful things, I at times felt an urge to hurt her in return. I would tell myself, "Why are you being nice to her when she is so mean to you? Be mean back. Make her pay."

I'm not proud that I felt this way. The truth: I was

probably more upset with *myself* for becoming so reactive. My adult self knows that she only said hurtful things because she was upset and hurting. This is how many of us cope. When I am in my adult self, I can hold a container for her emotions without the feeling of wanting to "make her pay." If only I had been in my adult self since she was born!

I came from the belief that, because I'm the parent, I should be respected. I now believe respect is earned. If I don't respect my son's or daughter's feelings or spirits, why should they respect mine? I also have a much clearer understanding that when we are reactive, it often stems from a need either to "grow ourselves up" or to heal a childhood wound.

TAKING RESPONSIBILITY

As parents, we imagine that our primary task is to raise our children until they are ready to function in the adult world. As a result of reading *The Conscious Parent*, I have come to see parenting differently. It's not so much about raising our children; it's also about our children providing the context in which we raise *ourselves* until we become emotionally mature. This is another way my children, in addition to my husband, have enabled me to shed my masks—especially after I took ownership of the ways they are each in my life to allow me to "grow myself up." I'm grateful to them (my kids are now in their twenties) for the growth I've experienced over the last dozen years. It's wonderful to see us all reaping the rewards for these difficult years. We have come a long way since family therapy.

Today, I'm able to parent in such a different way from when my son and daughter were young. I focus not on their plaster surface but on their gold interior. I'm able to serve as a mirror to reflect their inherent goodness. I tell my son how much I appreciate his honesty, courage, cooperativeness, and sense of adventure. I also appreciate that my daughter is creative, strong, and assertive while also being incredibly sweet. I no longer blame or shame them for the way they sometimes behave. It's not that I don't still worry about some of their more immature patterns, but I no longer expect them to please me or to be perfect the way I felt I was expected to be when I was a child.

I really noticed my growth when I prevented myself from falling into an old pattern a couple of years ago. It was my birthday, and when I first woke up, I didn't receive any birthday wishes. My family had clearly forgotten what day it was! The hours continued to pass, and still no birthday wishes. I felt unworthy, unlovable, and like I didn't matter, just like I often felt as a child.

I wanted to say something to my kids, to guilt them for forgetting. But when I paused first, I realized that was exactly what my mom used to do. At that moment, it dawned on me that I was acting like her, and I was grateful for the awareness and that I didn't publicly present my initial reaction. Had it been ten years prior,

I definitely would have guilted my kids. Thankfully, they eventually remembered it was my birthday, but had I said something earlier from a place of reactivity, it would have put a strain on our relationship.

I have learned to focus on what happens in myself when I react emotionally. And I have summoned the courage to have conversations with my family about things that used to be difficult for me to address.

Whenever my old patterns show up with my kids, because they do, I quickly identify the pattern, take responsibility for doing my healing work, then show up in a different way.

MAKING AMENDS

When my kids were younger, I didn't have the relationship with them I hoped for (have I mentioned that?) There were many times I behaved in ways I'm not proud of, but I truly didn't know that I was operating out of childhood patterns instead of what the present moment required of me.

I had a lot of guilt, fearing I couldn't protect my children from experiencing the pain I felt growing up. Though I no longer harbor that guilt, I do still feel sad about the early days when I failed to protect them. I say this simply to illustrate the huge way in which my parenting has evolved.

At one point many years ago, in an attempt to make amends, I shared with them how remorseful I felt. I said, "I am so sorry that I ever hurt you. I regret all the times I wasn't gentle, loving, understanding, and compassionate. I wish I hadn't been so critical, harsh, and blaming. I wish I could have been more nurturing and shared my heart with you."

I then added, "And I'm sorry for the times that I raged at you, screamed at you, and chose to control you. I wish that every time you messed up, I had said, 'It's okay, you'll get it in time.'" I hated that they had grown up in an environment where they, too, might have felt like they were expected to be perfect. I feared that they would grow up being as hard on themselves as I'd been on myself and would blame themselves for their screw ups.

My reason for sharing these stories with you is to make the point that we aren't supposed to be perfect moms. I tried to be a perfect mom, and clearly, I wasn't. No one is. The key is that we learn to take responsibility when we mess up and take action to do better. It's not about being hard on ourselves or shaming ourselves for the times we screwed up. It's about owning up to the fact that we made a mistake and then trying to be better.

Eliminating Stinking Thinking

Part of taking ownership is realizing that we each co-create our reality. In tandem, it's imperative to realize when we're allowing a past trauma to impact our present reality. It's also important to know when we are allowing our fear of the future to dictate our present.

I used to have a bad case of what I've heard referred to as "stinking-thinking." In essence, I was being negative more often than not. Our brains are wired to look for the negative. Many experts call this having a negativity bias, and it's how our ancestors, who dwelled in caves, kept themselves safe.

Today we don't have to look out for a bear around the corner, so we have to learn to override this part of our brain by creating new neural pathways, more positive ones. I don't want to be seen as a "Debbie downer," but when I can't control something, I become quite anxious. Having a desire to control things is perfectly normal; our brains are wired to move away from pain, toward pleasure, and we often think that by controlling events, we can avoid pain. Even though that sense of control is only an illusion, it somehow takes away the discomfort felt when faced with a difficult situation.

At times in my life, I've felt like I was losing my mind because no matter what I tried, I couldn't escape ruminating on thoughts of fear and worry. Whenever I was alone with my thoughts, the negative mental chatter was there. This is the mental prison I often speak of. One of the best decisions I made in the course of taking ownership of my patterns was acknowledging the pattern of stinking-thinking and beginning to find ways to live more in the present moment, which wasn't at all easy.

Dr. Joe Dispenza is a neuroscientist and bestselling author who teaches people how to change their minds in order to improve their lives. As Albert Einstein famously stated, "Doing the same thing over and over and expecting different results is the definition of insanity." Dispenza says if we want a new and different future, we have to change the way we think and, therefore, feel. Any time we change our thoughts and feelings, we change our present reality. We need to learn to watch for times when we allow old but familiar patterns to overlay our present, which can, in turn, predict our future.

I began to learn to catch myself whenever I fell back into the patterns and changed my thoughts. One of the ways I did this (and still do) is by reminding myself that there are infinite possibilities in the present moment, so there is no need to be fearful or worried about the future.

Another approach that's worked well for me is meditating on the feelings I want to embrace. I focus my attention on feeling grateful, free, calm, at ease, and peaceful. I remind myself of the saying "Energy flows where attention goes." If I want my life to be free, abundant, and joyful, but I am placing my attention on all the things I am worried about or the lack in my life, I'm not going to feel those joyful, abundant feelings I desire.

MINDSET MATTERS

Not long ago, I had COVID. The old me would have gone into total panic, quickly visualizing myself in the hospital on a ventilator. The reason I would have thought this way is completely understandable: I have an underlying health condition that makes me more susceptible to this virus. When COVID was at its worst, many of the people who were dying also had comorbidity, which didn't help my mindset.

However, when I had COVID this particular time, I practiced what I had learned from Joe Dispenza and focused on being grateful for my life. I put my attention on having a healthy body and feeling strong. I also took an antiviral, so that might have helped. But in two days, the COVID symptoms were gone, and I was playing tennis and boxing again within a week. That recovery speed wasn't my norm a couple of years ago.

My point is, our mindset makes a difference. It's true that where you place your attention impacts the reality you co-create with the universe. We are always manifesting, drawing in that which we are putting out. So why not focus on more of what you want in your life rather than what you don't want?

A while back, I decided that I wanted to focus on my health and lose a bit of weight. Rather than obsessing over counting calories and weighing myself every morning, I instead focused on eating mindfully. The weight came off automatically—maybe not immediately, but without nearly the effort I imagined it might require.

In order to create the life I desired, I needed to take ownership for making the necessary changes in my approach. What I wanted wasn't going to descend on me out of thin air. I had to do the work.

To create the life of my choosing, it helps to see my life as a garden. Within that garden, I have a variety of individual gardens. There's a health garden, relationship garden, business garden, and personal growth garden. Every day I nurture my gardens by doing a variety of things to help them grow. I begin my day with daily habits like meditation, journaling, and reading something motivational. I also make sure to work out most days. I try to plan each week so I am set up to eat healthy food, and I'm intentional about creating balance in my life by alternating between work and fun social events.

I also make sure to remove the weeds (negative thoughts, beliefs, and patterns). I've accepted that I need to regularly pick weeds while accepting they may never fully disappear. For the rest of my life, I will continue to work on any and all of my challenging areas. But most of the challenges that continue to arise, I meet head-on. I know that as long as I keep plugging away, I will be okay. I can't always control what the garden will produce, I can only control my part and then let nature take its course. Some of my gardens may not flourish exactly as I would like or in the timeframe I hope for, but that is the nature of life.

I have come to realize how amazingly life flows when I accept others as they are and life as it is. When I approach each day from a place of inner abundance, things happen spontaneously, often pleasantly surprising me. When we cultivate a practice of being in the present moment, we no longer live out a pattern from the past or fears about the future. We simply learn to live, one moment at a time.

PART III

WILLINGNESS TO FEEL TO HEAL

The Giant Sulk

Many of us pepper our days with upbeat moments, but deep down we're afraid to let ourselves feel too happy for fear we might be again disappointed. Rather than have an exuberant love of life wherein we are constantly awash with joy, we find ourselves imprisoned in a "giant sulk"—an underlying, ever-present feeling that we aren't enough. None of us escapes the sense—even if only occasionally—that being ourselves somehow isn't enough. This is why many of us feel driven to achieve, while others simply give up and function like bottom-feeding fish. The giant sulk feels like a low-grade fever of numbness, like you're merely existing and surviving. The pain buried deep below the surface keeps you from feeling fully alive.

This sulk, reinforced by whatever wounds were inflicted on us during childhood, can overwhelm us with debilitating sadness. There were days, if not weeks, when I felt as if I had plunged into a deep, dark abyss from which there was no escape. I told myself there was no bottom to my painful state and sometimes wondered if I needed medication. I know many others who have suffered from this same seemingly bottomless pit of pain. I promise you, there *is* a bottom, and you can find your way up from there.

Self-doubt is a primary driver of nearly every uncertainty, anxiety, and worry we experience. It's why we mask up in the first place. Beset with doubt about ourselves and our abilities—not to mention our capabilities—we spend our lives seeking to prove we are worthy. If enough damage was done in our younger years, we may simply consider ourselves outright *un*worthy.

The sore place in us is, by its very nature, beyond anything we can affect simply by trying to be more positive or optimistic. Therefore, the only way to heal this "giant sulk" is by going inward. We have to *feel* our pain if we are to heal it, which seems counterintuitive, because *feeling* the sulk is exactly opposite our desire! But doing so is a crucial step, because it's how we go from the mind into the heart, where the pain is trapped. The sulk can be transformed into a state of aliveness, of accepting, embracing, and loving ourselves.

Feeling my feelings wasn't something I'd ever been terribly good at. Identifying my feelings was never modeled for me, let alone experiencing or talking about them. But the biggest problem with pushing down our feelings is that the energy from those feelings stays stored in the body. I actually believe a key part of why I developed an autoimmune disease was that my body was screaming at me to heal from all of the pain I had spent years shoving down.

DON'T BE AFRAID TO FEEL YOUR FEELINGS

To heal from my long-standing patterns, I had to learn how to effectively feel my feelings as well as comfort the little girl inside who was afraid to rock the boat. Because I was never directly told by my parents that it wasn't okay to be angry, sad, or scared, it must have been something I picked up on energetically. I somehow felt that there was no space for me to have emotions. I also suspect that because it was so scary to witness others having big emotions, I was afraid to experience them for myself, and instead chose to squash them.

While I hated feeling all of my less-than-positive emotions, the one I detested most was fear. I was in a perpetual state of fear, and it dictated much of my life. From my teenage years on, my nervous system was, for the most part, locked in overdrive. I could barely access that feeling I'd long ago had at my aunt and uncle's lake house. My neck and shoulder muscles were constantly tight and tense, and if I paid close enough attention, I could sense my nervous system buzzing with anxious energy.

I wondered where this fear and anxiety came from. Both of my parents had experienced varying degrees of anxiety, so perhaps I absorbed some of it through osmosis. I believe that I inherited my mom's anxiety through the womb as well. After all, she had so much unhealed pain of her own.

In addition, I'm aware of a defining early moment for me, one in which I experienced sheer fear and panic. I was five, and while playing with my cousins and pretending to be eating dinner while playing house, I accidentally inhaled a pine tree needle. It was lodged in my throat, and I started choking and vomiting blood. I was so scared, sure that I would die.

It didn't help that the adults around me were panicking as well. I clearly remember my mom freaking out, not knowing what to do. Shouting for others to help, I think she too believed I was going to die. I continued to vomit blood for what seemed like hours, and when I saw the blood in the toilet it scared me to death. Plus, I couldn't breathe well with this pine needle wedged in my throat. Eventually, my dad grabbed me and was ready to rush me to the hospital. As we were running out the door, the piece of pine needle came up. It took a long time for me to recover from this. In fact, I had a phobia of vomiting for many years.

While experiencing this was traumatizing, and likely would be for anyone, the most impactful part was that, after the event, no one talked with me to see if I was okay. Not one adult said to me, "That must have been so scary for you. Are you okay?" No one held me and reassured me that I would be alright, which, in hindsight, I clearly needed. I pushed my feelings aside and simply carried on, because I didn't want to upset my mom, and I worried that perhaps it was "wrong" to have these emotional needs.

When I was a teenager, my mom and I had a huge argument. From what I recall, I was speaking up about something I believed to be true. She didn't like what I said and let me know it. Since I was in adolescence, I had a little more rebellion in me at times, and on this occasion, I chose to stand up for myself and my beliefs. It got ugly, and we were both screaming at one another. I was infuriated because I felt like she was discounting my feelings and telling me how wrong I was for feeling the way I did.

I hadn't done anything "wrong," per se. I just said something she didn't agree with. I can't remember a time before this one when I was so angry. In the moment, I hated her, and I shouted, "Fuck You!", stormed out of the house, hopped on my bike, and rode around town crying my eyes out. I spent the whole night in a dugout at a baseball field, scared and lonely. So many times, I wanted to go home, but I was so angry with my mom for dismissing me and discounting my feelings that I stayed there, freezing and trying to sleep on a bench. My parents tried to find me, but it never occurred to them that I would be in a dugout at a baseball field, so they never looked there.

After having experiences like this, we often learn to invalidate our feelings and brush them off as being no big deal. But our emotions are present for a reason. They are trail markers, indicating where we need to heal old, unprocessed pain.

Many times in my youth, I used food to numb the pain I was so afraid of feeling. I remember once sitting at the kitchen table, I was likely only eight years old, having just witnessed a big argument between my mom and one of my cousins. I couldn't stand the yelling and slamming of doors. Feeling scared and anxious, I went to the refrigerator once things started calming down, grabbed the milk, and then grabbed a new package of Oreos from the pantry and sat back down. One after another, I dunked the Oreos into the milk and shoved them in my mouth. After the first two, I don't think I even tasted them because I was eating so mindlessly. I just wanted to shove them in as fast as I could, hoping (subconsciously, of course) it would take away the pain. After some time passed, I looked down and realized I ate a whole row of the cookies. I promise you, it didn't take the pain away, but in the moment, it soothed my anxiety.

If you also dismiss your feelings, as I did, those feelings will haunt you, causing you to experience numbness, addictive behaviors, sadness, or depression. And the longer you battle the feelings by pushing them down, the more difficult it will be to heal and come into wholeness.

Many who grew up in my generation weren't encouraged to feel their feelings. If we were sad, we were told to paste a smile on our faces. If we wanted to jump for joy, we were scolded and ordered to calm down. We were taught that we should learn to sit still instead of skipping and running when we felt like it. Boys should not cry, and girls should stay out of the mud. Children shouldn't be what children naturally are.

The problem with this type of social conditioning is that what we were being told was: "Don't have feelings"; "Don't be human." What we needed was for our caregivers to acknowledge what we were feeling, whether sadness, anger, joy, fear, or frustration. We then needed permission to *feel* and *express* those emotions. We didn't know how to process big emotions. We needed our caregivers to hold us tenderly and compassionately whenever we felt overwhelmed by our feelings. I have had to learn to cultivate being gentle and compassionate with myself because I didn't have anyone who could truly hold me and be tender with me. Heck, I wasn't even tender with myself, so why would I expect someone to be tender with me? I longed to have someone be gentle with me, but the problem with craving that was, I was always seeking "out there" for that someone. What I really needed to learn was how to show up for myself. (Sidenote: If you are looking for a great book that focuses specifically on how to do this, step-by-step, check out *Show Up For Yourself: A Guide to Inner Growth and Awareness* by Janet Philbin). This was the most important and pivotal part of my healing journey. I had to be the adult for that scared little girl inside me. I had to be tender and gentle with her and provide her with the safety she longed for.

HEALING THE WOUNDED SELF

Because I was not savvy at identifying my feelings or knowing the source of my pain, I often overreacted as deep layers of old pain were continuously stirred up. So it wasn't surprising when I found myself in a particularly upsetting and memorable situation with my husband. He made an off-the-cuff comment about doing something to help our son, who was, at the time, having fun with his friends. I don't recall the exact request my son made, but I recollect it being something simple, like starting a fire so he and his friends could toast marshmallows. My husband was busy and didn't want to stop what he was doing to help out, so he made a remark and sounded irritated. I was nearby and could sense that my son felt badly about the way his dad responded. I intuited that he felt guilty for having bothered him.

The reason I went ballistic was that my husband's remark triggered a wound dating back to my childhood. As I've mentioned, my mother (surely inadvertently) used guilt to control me, constantly throwing in my face all that she had done for me. My mom was generous. She did a lot for me and made sure I always had whatever I needed. The issue was, whenever she was upset with me for not doing what she wanted me to do, she made it a point to remind me of all the things she'd done for me. She came from the belief that relationships are transactional. The way in which she threw in my face all that she had done for me inflicted a wound that marked me as "bad" for not doing exactly what she demanded of me. This reinforced the original wound that shouted, "You are undeserving." I felt it wasn't safe to receive what I wished for, knowing it could later be thrown back at me.

In another example, my parents paid my entire college tuition because they didn't want me to graduate with loans. This wasn't easy for them to do. My dad made pretty good money, but it was still a stretch to pay for the private school I attended.

My career as a high school teacher lasted six years before my son was born. On several occasions after leaving teaching in order to be a stay-at-home mom, my mother made underhanded comments about having paid for my college, only to have me give up teaching to be a mom. The way I interpreted her comments was that I had wasted her money, and she was upset by it. I'd learned from her and countless others that gifts are not always given freely and often have strings attached.

When my husband made that comment to my son, while I initially lashed out, it didn't take long for me to recognize that it had awakened a deep pain within me, and it was time to confront this wound, a wound that had been stored in my body for years.

After I allowed myself the space to confront this pain and feel the feelings I'd buried, an inner peace followed. From a place of calm, I was able to have a more conscious conversation with my husband to explain why I reacted the way I did.

Several years back, a close and dear friend ended a ten-year friendship with me after I spoke up and told her how I truly felt about the direction our relationship was headed. I was careful to share from my heart. I didn't blame or attack her. But in spite of my efforts, she felt attacked and became defensive over the phone, screaming before hanging up on me. I haven't heard from her since.

This experience reinforced my belief that whenever I speak up for myself and assert my needs, others will get angry and abandon me. When someone we value pulls away and we don't know why, we often conclude that we did something wrong. We blame ourselves when another is upset with us or no longer wishes to be part of our life. These wounds are unpleasant on their own, but when added to the layers of history, they only reinforce the pain of our earliest days.

If you resonate with what I'm saying, it's likely that you also experienced a deep emotional wound in your earliest days. Your initial insecurity was perhaps later reinforced when, as a growing child, you weren't invited to a birthday party. Or maybe your best friend stopped being friends with you, choosing instead to cozy up to someone else. Or perhaps your caregivers' use of guilt made you feel that you were less-than or even "bad."

This deeper pain tends to be reawakened during times when it feels like life is against us. A death, a divorce, being jilted, losing a pet, or a business reversal can bring buried pain to the surface. When that happens, it's important to feel the pain and give it the love and nurturing it needs to fully heal. Don't suppress it by squashing or ignoring it.

My newfound ability to feel my feelings in order to heal was a strong catalyst in enabling me to go from prison to paradise. Paradise is knowing that I don't have to live a life of emotional powerlessness, as I did as a child. Paradise is knowing that there is a way to show up gracefully in my relationships. Paradise is freedom!

Returning briefly to the metaphor of dredging, in order to continue to peel back the layers and heal more and more over time, I didn't dredge my river just once. As did the Army Corps of Engineers with the lower Mississippi, I discovered that my life is more likely to flow smoothly if I dredge continually. In the early days of healing, being miserable was a comfortable feeling I easily returned to if I skipped even a few days of dredging. Even today, I still need to dredge by attending to my childhood wounds whenever I am confronted with the sludge that muddies my inner flow.

I have learned that the way to keep my energy flowing free and clear is to love myself by accepting myself in every situation life sends my way, and the only way I can do that is by continuing to heal my childhood pain and trauma.

8

Understanding Emotional Reactivity

Infants quite readily express rage, jealousy, and possessiveness. Even in the most loving and supportive environments, they scream, wail, and pout if they don't get what they want. They are by nature narcissistic, indulging in emotional outbursts to secure what they want. But this doesn't work terribly well the older we get.

If we wish to respond to triggering situations with emotional maturity, we first have to understand where our emotional reactivity comes from. You may wonder why you are emotionally reactive at times. Perhaps you blame your parents for the way you "act out." You may believe that your parents tainted your innate goodness and, in the process, *made* you emotionally reactive. This belief is a cop out. Our parents didn't cause our reactivity; they shaped it. The particular *form* our childish outbursts take is partly modeled after those who raised us, but the outbursts themselves didn't begin with them. We came into the world fully equipped to react.

Blaming our parents for our behavior, as if we would have remained pristine had they not messed us up, doesn't help us manage our inborn narcissism and the emotional reactivity that fuels it. Unless we were taught otherwise by parents who were conscious of their own behaviors, we demanded to have our way and wanted what we wanted "this minute." As toddlers, we often pitched fits, screaming at anyone within earshot. As four- and five-year-olds, we continued to do this in the park, on a plane, or in the grocery store. Many of us still act like toddlers from time to time, railing at another, blaming them. One only has to hear about the tantrums recently thrown in the presence of airline attendants, sometimes even forcing planes to divert, to recognize this to be true.

The majority of us don't enjoy the kind of connection we secretly long for because we haven't learned to nurture a level of emotional maturity that enables us to connect with others in a meaningful way. We subconsciously choose who we become close to because they reflect those aspects of ourselves that are as yet undeveloped. Their behavior feels familiar and therefore "safe." Through interaction with each other, however, we see the many ways in which we have yet to grow up, if we are open to that awareness. And if we want our connection with others to improve, we need to learn to respond, not overreact.

In order to do this, we first must become aware when we are feeling triggered by another's behavior. Then, we need to pause and check in with ourselves to see if an old childhood wound is being reinfected. If that is the case, it is our responsibility to give our child self what is needed in that moment. Once we have met the unmet need, we can respond from our adult self rather than overreact from our child self.

Parents fail their children when they themselves are run by their emotions, reinforcing unproductive emotional patterns that come naturally instead of derailing them. I have learned to see my father and mother in much of my behavior. But I also see how I developed my own ways of reacting, and in some ways, outdid them. After all, our parents did the best they could with what they knew while carrying their own pain from not having their own needs met.

I can easily recall countless times when I "lost it" in front of my children. Once, when my children were young and we were at Disney World, it was the end of the day and we were looking for the car in the parking lot. I couldn't remember where I parked, and it was late and dark. I started to panic, scared that we would be stranded. As my kids complained because they were tired and didn't want to continue aimlessly wandering through the gigantic parking lot, I snapped at them. I was losing more patience and getting more nervous by the minute. I couldn't find any attendants to help us, and in the pitch dark, I lost total control of my emotions and was in fight or flight mode. As a result, I scared my kids. I believe that witnessing multiple instances of this type of behavior from me conditioned them to overreact in stressful circumstances.

My own worry and anxiety prevented me from being present to the fact that my kids were exhausted from a long day in the park and may have been scared as well. If I'd been able to stay calm and collected, I would have gone over to my kids, bent down to their eye level, reassured them that we would find the car, and acknowledged how tired they were. I would then have given them a hug and carried on to find the car. But since I wasn't in control of my emotions, I couldn't remain present to what they were feeling.

Today, I am able to be present with them in harrowing situations because I learned how to settle *myself* whenever I am anxious or worried about them. That's not to say that I'm perfect, because there are certainly times when I feel more anxious than normal about something one of my kids is doing. But I quickly recognize that I am projecting and use meditation or my mantras to settle myself and let go of my worry. As a result, our relationships are much healthier.

An important role for parents and caregivers to play is modeling self-control. After all, part of growing up is learning how to govern our emotions instead of being governed by them.

Expressing authentic feelings is different from having emotional reactivity. To see the difference, imagine yourself on a date with your spouse on Valentine's Day. You enjoy a wonderfully romantic dinner together and are both looking forward to a passionate night in the bedroom. On the way home, the topic of whether you should spend next Thanksgiving with one set of parents or the other comes up, and you end up arguing. A little while later, instead of being close in the way you anticipated, you find yourselves on opposite sides of the bed. What are you experiencing as you lie there? Certainly distance, undoubtedly disappointment, and most likely resentment. The last thing you want right now is for your partner to speak to you, let alone touch you. "Stay on your own side of the bed" is the silent message, loud and clear.

This is a moment to ask yourself whether that's the truth of what you're feeling. If you listen beneath the voices in your head, the ones that are perhaps encouraging you to emotionally react by either shutting down or lashing out, you may hear a quite different message. Deeper than and distinct from your surface-level emotions, you may be surprised to notice a deep longing to reconnect but feel imprisoned by emotional reactivity, reinforced by the barrage of distancing thoughts your mind feeds you that don't allow you to reach out. You may also wish your spouse would reach out—though if he did, you might be emotionally reactive, spurning his overtures and turning away from him.

Unlike the voices in your head, the underlying feeling of wanting to connect is calm, quiet, and not nearly as compulsive as your emotions. There is nothing insistent, nothing driven about it. It's just... *there*.

This desire to connect originates from an awareness that you are already connected at a deep level. It's a desire to *re*connect. The feeling springs from a "knowing" to which you were resistant in the moment. You realize you are going to make up; you just aren't yet ready to set aside your emotional reactivity.

THE POWER OF THE PAUSE

When I began connecting my emotional reactivity to patterns of behavior dating back to childhood, I recognized I needed to practice closing the gap between venting my emotion and recognizing I was reacting. I eventually became adept at pausing when I felt anger arising, which opened my ability to interrupt the impulse to react. Eventually, I learned to close the gap between being triggered and stopping the resulting emotion in its tracks. We can use this insight to better understand how we can get a grip on ourselves in emotionally reactive moments.

I had never thought of watching myself, observing my reactions in real time, but it would become a valuable step toward more mature behavior. At first, it took me several days to acknowledge when I was acting from a lifelong pattern. But as I became more practiced at observing myself, the time between losing it and understanding what was happening grew shorter.

One day, though I couldn't stop my emotion, I was able to watch myself while a reaction was in progress. I saw how it arose and possessed me. Upon walking into the kitchen and observing an ungodly mess, I immediately experienced the familiar feeling of how "wrong" the children were for making this mess. A rush of anger gushed up in my chest, and my throat, shoulders, and arms tightened as my stomach knotted. I was aware for the first time that my feeling of "rightness" was, in truth, an emotional reaction.

This was an important breakthrough, because until then I had justified my anger as an appropriate and rational response. On this occasion, however, I knew, while I was actively losing it, that I was reacting. From that point on, whenever I felt anger, I remained calm long enough to ask myself, "Could it be that I'm not being rational, that I'm reacting?"

For a brief moment before being engulfed by my narcissistic emotions, I sensed I didn't *have* to react. I suddenly saw that I had a choice. I could either let the emotion take me over, or I could calm myself.

This is one reason I choose to incorporate meditation into my day. It enables me to avoid getting hooked on reacting the way I used to. Meditation has helped me pause as I practice watching my thoughts without reacting or judging them when I am in a relaxed, calm state. The more I practice and build this muscle, the more equipped I am to hold onto my emotions when in the heat of the moment.

Of course, my emotions occasionally overwhelm my true feelings, even today. When someone attempts to control me, silence me, or shame me, it triggers my childhood wound of unworthiness. But now, I can pause long enough to go inward and soothe my child self. From this place, I can choose to respond with emotional maturity.

If we want to come into wholeness to be our true selves, it is imperative to heal our childhood wounds and incorporate mindfulness into our lives. Some may argue that you can change your life just by changing your thoughts and your mindset. Some may argue that the key to changing your life is healing your past. I believe that both need to occur in order to fully heal and come into wholeness.

PART IV

EMBRACING OUR CHILD SELF

Reparenting Yourself

When we feel rejected or abandoned if someone doesn't meet our needs, instead of being angry and blaming, we need to learn how to go inward and give our sulking self the nurturing it needs. This is what it means to reparent ourselves. It isn't our adult self that feels rejected or abandoned, it's our child self. It's a wound that was created when we were children. When this wound becomes infected, it oozes in the form of emotional reactivity. It's up to us to clean and heal it, removing the infection. Whenever we feel triggered, our adult self must be able to soothe our child self. This is an important step in learning to regulate our emotions.

The only way to truly heal our childhood wounds so we don't continue to live out our patterns is to do the inner work in the present. We heal our past by using current situations as they arise and taking new action in order to have new outcomes.

In the past, whenever I was triggered by someone or some situation, I would react from my childhood wounds. My past was overlaying the present. Today, I do my best to pause and calm myself. It may take only a few minutes, sometimes longer, to go inward and nurture the wound that was triggered. I put balm on the wound by telling my child self that I am here for her and will not abandon her. I remind her that she is worthy and safe. Once my child self feels seen and heard, I return to homeostasis. Then I come back to the situation that triggered me and choose to respond rather than react.

I still encounter issues that upset me, but I now allow myself to deeply feel them so I can release whatever emotion I am feeling at the moment. When a feeling of pain arises, I have learned to breathe through it and collapse it. It's like building a muscle; I have to be diligent to repeatedly be able to bring myself back to a calm state. After much practice, I am now powerful enough to do so.

SHOW UP FOR YOURSELF

I recently had a colonoscopy and subsequent surgery. Afterwards, I didn't feel well. Three days post-surgery I was worse—lightheaded, dizzy, and weak. I was close to fainting, and my heart rate was irregular.

I finally decided to go to urgent care. Because we

were celebrating my mother-in-law's birthday, this wasn't an easy decision. My old pattern of putting others' needs ahead of my own was surfacing. I tormented myself for over two hours, feeling worse by the minute. I kept telling myself to "suck it up," but I was scared and on the verge of calling 911. My old patterns were emerging. I didn't want to make a scene or ruin everyone's good time, which is classic people-pleasing behavior. I worried that I might be making a "mountain out of a molehill." What if this turned out to be nothing and everyone's good time was ruined by me?

While at urgent care, waiting for the doctor to return with the blood work results, I sensed that my husband was impatient and didn't want to stay. I must have asked three times whether he was okay. Imagine, I was the one who was sick, but there I was, worrying about his feelings! I took his behavior personally, when the reality is that he's frequently impatient when it comes to things like waiting in the doctor's office. His behavior had nothing to do with me.

I don't claim that our old patterns will go away entirely as a result of doing inner healing. As you can see, some of my old patterns still surface now and then, and I have done quite a lot of healing work. But I can say with confidence that you will become equipped at recognizing it more quickly when these patterns show up. From there, you will know how to take care of yourself and respond from a healthier point of view. Once we arrived home, I deconstructed what had occurred. I discovered that I had resurrected an old pattern that told me I wasn't "enough" and shouldn't expect my husband to wait with me. I had an outdated belief that it was my responsibility to support everyone else and not to expect others to support me.

I also came to an awareness that I had abandoned myself. I allowed my scared child self to drive the bus. That part of myself was frightened she was going to die. My adult self was nowhere to be found, and my child self was left feeling alone. I needed the mature, rational part of myself to show up and reassure me that we can get through hard things. Because I had been practicing healing my inner self for a long time, I knew that I needed to offer compassion and reassurance to the part of me that was wounded and scared—the same part of me that was scared she would die from having swallowed a pine needle so many years prior.

I eventually arrived at a place where I'm able to reassure myself that I am worthy of others being there for me, and it's okay to ask for what I need, knowing that if the other says no, I am equipped to be there for myself.

My initial go-to response was to sweep how I felt about my husband's behavior under the rug, which was also an unhealthy pattern from childhood. Instead, I confessed to him that I'd taken his actions personally while assuring him that what had occurred was less about him and more about my feelings when I was growing up. He heard what I was saying, and it allowed for a moment of connection between us.

There is freedom that comes from being attuned to your patterns and choosing to respond from a healthier, more empowered place. It may not happen overnight or even as quickly as you'd like, but with practice and patience, you'll get there.

SELF-COMPASSION IS THE BALM

A couple of years ago, as Independence Day rolled around, I reflected on how far I had come in my personal sense of independence as well as my ability to relate to others. As I sat and drank my tea, I celebrated my growth and newfound ability to be true to myself in any and all situations.

For most of my life, I'd been unable to celebrate myself. I had such a hard time seeing my goodness. Whenever people complimented me, I didn't believe them. Because I felt unworthy, I had a hard time accepting praise. This is why I pushed myself to be better. I was looking at the yardstick in front of me, not the one behind me. This deeply rooted pattern still at times compels me to be hard on myself, driving me to be "more." I feel I have to be uber competent, the do-it-all woman, saying yes to so much because that's what I've always done. It's a heavy load to carry.

I like to use mountain-based analogies when I reflect on my life. For a lot of my life, I felt like I was climbing straight up a very steep mountain, carrying a heavy backpack that was nearly pulling me backward. I now like to imagine that I take breaks along the way, setting up camp and toasting marshmallows. Taking the time to rest doesn't mean that we stop climbing altogether and abandon our responsibilities. It means that we take time throughout our days to nurture our mind, body, and spirit.

If I decide to skip writing my newsletter or pause on recording my podcast for a while, it's okay. I finally realized that I was putting pressure on my child self to be perfect and meet my unrealistic expectations. I was, in essence, bullying her when I needed to give myself grace and compassion by allowing myself to ease up.

When I recognize that the perfectionism pattern is showing up again, I nurture my child self by being gentler and more compassionate with her. I remind myself that no one is going to yell at me or be upset—and if they are, it's too bad. As long as I am doing my best, that's all that matters. The same is true for you. As long as you are doing your best, you're doing great.

My deeper self knows that I am like the ocean; nothing can hurt or destroy me. I am that expansive and powerful, and you are too! My soul knows that the chatter and noise in my mind is nothing more than the waves of the ocean, sometimes calm and at other times boisterous.

If you struggle with giving yourself grace when your old patterns rear their heads, it might be helpful to seek the support of a trusted friend, coach, or therapist to assist you with this until you are able to regularly engage in self-compassion more fully.

Integrating Our Whole Selves

An important part of the healing process is learning to accept all the parts of ourselves that we judge, criticize, and cut ourselves off from, acting as if the parts that we dislike don't even exist. Don't worry, I'm not asking you to love every part of you that you wish didn't exist, I'm simply inviting you to allow them to just be. Over time, you will likely get to a place where you love all of yourself, the light and the dark. Living from wholeness means being able to accept and integrate *all* parts of ourselves without judging and criticizing. It means we're no longer willing to be at war with any aspect of ourselves.

In my case, one part of me I'd long criticized lingered longer than others: my relationship with my body. As documented in the Netflix special, "Miss

Americana," pop star Taylor Swift candidly shared her feelings about opening the shutters to her life of fame by delivering an uncommon level of emotional honesty through her music. When the documentary premiered at the Sundance Film Festival, one of the less nasty remarks made about her was, "She's too skinny. It bothers me." It also bothered the star herself. In one of the most revealing and surprising segments of the documentary, she talks about her struggle with an eating disorder, admitting she starved herself to become thin.

Swift said that her "relationship with food was exactly the same psychology that I applied to everything else in my life: If I was given a pat on the head, I registered that as good. If I was given a punishment, I would register that as bad." She added, "You register that enough times, and you just start to accommodate everything towards praise and punishment, including your own body."

Said the filmmaker, "It's incessant, and I can say this as a woman: It's amazing to me how people are constantly like 'You look skinny' or 'You've gained weight.' People you barely know say this to you. And it feels awful, and you can't win either way. So I think it's really brave to see someone who is a role model for so many girls and women be really honest about that."

Swift said, "If you're thin enough, then you don't have that ass that everybody wants. But if you have enough weight on you to have an ass, your stomach isn't flat enough." As she became aware of the no-win scenario, it caused her to "go into a real shame/hate spiral."

"Miss Americana" was popular because it offered us a glimpse at Swift's real self—behind her masks—in a way that we had never seen before. Prior to that, she withheld many details about her personal life and only focused on her music. The documentary quite possibly helped her reach even greater heights by letting people into her personal orbit.

After fighting an eating disorder for decades, I started working with a registered dietician to help me achieve food freedom. I'd been a compulsive overeater since I was a little girl, and I was tired of being controlled by food.

With the dietitian's guidance, I learned several tools to help me eat more mindfully, such as eating only when I'm hungry and stopping when I'm pleasantly full. About ten weeks into our work together, I had a binge episode. Rather than being gentle and compassionate with myself, I was exceptionally harsh. It took an entire lifetime to get to where I was, yet I expected to heal myself in ten weeks. There was a nonstop internal pressure to be perfect. I normally eat five meals a day. If I did well during four of those and ate compulsively and mindlessly during one, I would beat myself up. I failed to see that recovery of a chronic condition is a process, with success waxing and waning.

Another long-standing pattern of mine has been judging my body. Anytime I'd pass by a mirror or window and see my reflection, I'd find something to criticize. I hated the way my butt, thighs, and stomach looked in the mirror and rarely identified anything positive about my body. I know this goes back to my experiences during puberty, and for some reason, I had the hardest time healing this specific part of me. Part of the work I did with Sarah, the registered dietician, included working on my body image. I am deeply grateful for that work with her. She taught me so much and helped guide me to a place where I could finally accept my body as it is. I recently had an epiphany that the mere idea of wanting to lose weight is essentially me just wanting to get rid of parts of myself.

In order for me to heal, I had to accept all parts of myself, including the body parts I disapproved of. I now feel more of a soft acceptance toward my body. It's time to embrace all of my parts exactly as they are, and if I decide that I want to tone what I have to improve my overall wellbeing, I will continue to weight train. This is a completely different energy than wanting to change myself because I loathe the way I look. I don't know if I will ever love the way my butt or hips look, but I am no longer willing to be at war with myself over it.

Women and young girls need to cease hating themselves because their looks don't measure up to some ideal standard. Although the standard of beauty is changing in our society, there is still an undertone that thin, tall, light skin, and blonde hair are idolized, whereas in other cultures, being larger and more voluptuous is more accepted. It's all a matter of perspective, so why not change the way we perceive ourselves?

EMBRACING YOUR IMPERFECTIONS

We all face the fear of being judged, along with worrying about being classified a "bad" person, but there's no need to let this fear dominate your life. It's a common experience and one we need to face with compassion.

We all have moments when we second-guess our actions and worry what others might think. We each have quirks and imperfections. The trick is to realize that these aspects of ourselves can be used to assist us in becoming who we truly are. When we embrace our quirks without fear or hesitation, they naturally evolve into assets.

Teddy Roosevelt said, "It's not the critic who counts; not the man who points out how the strong man stumbles, or where the doer of deeds could have done them better. The credit belongs to the man who is actually in the arena, whose face is marred by dust and sweat and blood; who strives valiantly; who errs, who comes short again and again; who spends himself in a worthy cause; who at best knows in the end the triumph of high achievement, and who at the worst, if he fails at least fails while daring greatly, so that his place shall never be with those cold and timid souls who neither know victory nor defeat."

Whenever I find myself worrying about others judging me, I remind myself of this quote. If the person judging me isn't in the arena, I don't give their judgments any weight.

Having said this, I'm more than aware that overcoming the fear of judgment isn't a switch that can instantly be flipped. I sometimes have trouble letting go of judging myself because my inner critic protects the way I was raised. I need to remind myself that it's okay if I don't have it all together all the time, and sometimes, I even allow myself to be a complete mess. It's part of being imperfect.

It took many years for me to get to a place where I didn't care what others thought of me. It's a deeply ingrained pattern for a perfectionist. Honestly, it's still difficult at times. Don't think for a moment that I don't worry about what others will think when they read this book! I worry whether people will like it or whether they'll judge me for the stories I'm sharing. But when that inner dialogue gets loud, I have the skills to remind myself that the only true thing that matters is my opinion of myself. Being in that place of "knowing" that I am worthy no matter what is validation of how much I've healed and a reminder that the goal is to lead a more authentic, fulfilled life, free from the constraints of what others think.

KNOW THAT YOU'RE ENOUGH

When many of us experience an inner void, we believe the solution is being with a certain person, having certain things, or receiving a specific degree of recognition.

If you were to look at my life from the outside, you would likely think that I "have it all." I have long been afraid of being judged for what I have been blessed with. I was raised to believe I needed to be humble, which meant that I imagined wealthy people as being "bad" in some way. In addition, I was always mindful of how others might feel, and I perceived that if I shared my good fortune, it might make them feel negatively. I wondered why I felt a void inside myself for so many years when my life seemed so great.

Even though I may appear to "have it all," I spent most of my life feeling like I was in a barren desert. I didn't believe I was a good enough daughter, friend, sister, cousin, teacher, mother, or wife. Regardless of the fact that I tried so hard to be perfect and please all of these people, I had a deep sense that I was not measuring up. If you were to survey any of these people, they would probably say that I am a good person they're grateful to have in their lives. But the sad reality was that, for many years, I didn't believe any of these things to be true. Having been denied the opportunity to nurture and develop my true self growing up, that sense of inner wholeness was missing. The saying "Money can't buy happiness" turned out to be true.

Self-doubt is a poison that can permeate every part of your life. It can impact your belief in yourself at work, as a partner, parent, child, or friend as well as in your ability to create the life you want. It's one of the primary reasons we play small and don't take risks.

Be aware of your inner dialogue. Do you tell yourself "I can" or "I can't"? It's not about being anxious and attaching to a desired outcome; it's about knowing that you can get yourself through anything. Keep in mind that we're supposed to feel uncomfortable leaning into discomfort. This is the nature of venturing beyond our comfort zones. But learn to create a space between your inner critic and your authentic self, and remember that the inner critic is nothing more than a voice in your head.

It came as a shock to realize that the emptiness I'd long experienced was nothing more than a mirage. I had simply lost touch with my core sense of self. The way forward was to do the inner work and heal from my patterns so I could remove my masks and let my true self re-emerge. As I healed more and more, I reunited with that core sense of who I am, and consequently, my life began to change.

I no longer feel I have to collapse in front of the TV in the evenings as my mom did when I was growing up. She was so exhausted from attending to the needs of everyone, and all she wanted to do was sit and watch "Blue Bloods" with a bag of chips. I repeated that pattern for years. These days, I slow down instead of rushing to check tasks off my to-do list. I savor them, infusing them with presence, aware that my body only exists in the present moment. I am learning to listen to it when it says yes or no. And I've finally made peace with the fact that deep down, I am enough—more than enough—and always have been.

LOVING YOURSELF UNCONDITIONALLY

Everything felt like such a big deal in my formative years. My behavior was always judged, and making mistakes was unacceptable. I learned that getting things "right" was all-important, and doing so meant that I was a "good" person. Many of us were taught that if we spilled a glass of milk, it was a major issue. If we were late coming home after playing with our friends, we were shamed.

My inner critic is still at times harsh with me, and although it's gentler than it was in years past, it still compels me to do more, be more, push harder. It also alerts me that it's not okay to take my foot off the pedal. But I've learned to change my approach of forcing myself to feel good all the time. I realize that there will be times when I feel like crap, especially when I need to heal another layer of my childhood pain, and I've learned to love myself unconditionally, no matter how I am feeling or the way I behave.

To help me quiet my inner critic, I remind myself of a quote from Swami Kripalu: "My beloved child, break your heart no longer. Each time you judge yourself, you break your own heart. You stop feeding on the love which is the wellspring of your own vitality. The time has come, your time to live, to celebrate, to see the goodness that you are..." This hit me hard, and a deep sense of grief washed over me as I realized how I repeatedly break my own heart each time I listen to my inner critic. Loving myself unconditionally was a challenge; it was such an ingrained pattern to be harsh with myself. However, I didn't want my kids to be harsh with themselves, and if I've learned anything, it's that we'll pass down these patterns if we aren't careful. If I wanted to be a cycle breaker, I would have to learn how to love myself, no matter what.

I increasingly feel reunited with the person I was born to be. One tool that I use to help me love myself unconditionally is a guided meditation through which I imagine my child self fitting in the palm of my hand. I then place my hand on my heart and imagine her resting there. Doing this meditation has allowed me to integrate that part of myself that was wounded but also the part of me that, without inhibition, flipped off the monkey bars. It allows my child self to be reunited with my adult self. As a consequence, I enjoy a deep inner peace along with feelings of aliveness and expansiveness.

LIVE FROM WHOLENESS

When you do the healing work and integrate the wounded parts of yourself, your life begins to shift in a magical way. You start to live and love from a place of wholeness. Another way of understanding the concept of coming into wholeness includes the concept of desire. When I speak of desire in this context, I'm referring to a love of life.

Love is the good feelings about ourselves seeking to exercise themselves by connecting with others. When we love someone, we want to share life with them and do nice things for them—not because we can't stand being without them, but because being with them enables us to enjoy our own wonderful self more fully.

When we openly care about our own precious selves, we also care deeply for individuals who participate with us in the adventure of becoming who we are. Therefore, the deepest demonstration of love I can offer another is my presence. And I can only offer my presence when I come from my wholeness.

The more we heal our patterns, take ownership for being the person we want to be, create safety for our child self, and integrate all parts of ourselves, the more we feel like a whole person. The more whole and healed we feel, the more present we are.

Recently, I've noticed that when I'm taking my walks, I am more attuned to the sounds of the birds and the sight of the trees, flowers, and little animals scurrying around. I feel so connected to the moment, and as a result, I feel truly alive. That low-grade fever of numbness I used to experience has disappeared.

It's amazing to feel so connected to the present moment. When I tap into that feeling, I know I'm tapping into something greater than myself. It's my essence, my true nature. It's hard to even put into words, but it's definitely the feeling I had at my aunt and uncle's lake house—the feeling of being connected to Source. And it's only possible because I am now in my wholeness, no longer living or loving from the wounded part of me.

As I free myself from the unrealistic expectations I placed on myself to be everything to everyone, I become more openhearted. Not only do I place fewer expectations on myself but I also expect less from others. I have fully released my husband from my need for him to care for my emotional needs. I no longer hold an expectation that he or our relationship has to look or be a certain way. I have surrendered, and as a result, there is more space for things to naturally shift between us. As my energy changed because of the healing work, my husband no longer feels pressure from me to change who he is. I no longer send the message that who he is or how he shows up is wrong or bad. I allow him to just be himself, and I can do that because I am allowing myself to be who *I* am. All of this has created a newfound ease and flow between us.

I assure you, if there's some part of your life that you're trying to fix or an area where you're striving to get a certain outcome, you're trying to control—and likely force—an outcome, which never works. Letting go and surrendering is the key. Just to be clear, surrendering does not mean being submissive or being a doormat. It means accepting reality as it is. You can still have desires, wishes and wants, and you can take action toward them, but you let go of any attachment to the results. There's so much peace and joy in living from this place. I am by no means saying it's easy to do; it took me a long time to finally get this. But now that I do understand, there's no going back. That I promise!

I am no longer the person who was, for so long, accustomed to wearing masks. I am coming into my wholeness more every day, freer than ever, experiencing the peace and stillness I once knew when hanging from the monkey bars or staring at my reflection in the lake at my aunt and uncle's house.

I see more clearly that I co-created my misery in my relationships. Was it okay for others to manipulate me and project their baggage onto me? No. But the way I reacted was on me. Reacting from a place of victimhood was the dance I was accustomed to, and I had to heal before I could join in a new dance. Only then could I take off my masks and unhook from old patterns. That's how I went from my prison to paradise.

PART V

RADICAL RESPONSIBILITY

Learning How to Communicate

In any relationship—whether with a partner, friend, family member, or colleague—open communication is an essential component of sharing our lives with each other. It's also a powerful tool for healing wounds that may exist between ourselves and the people we love. When we are able to express our thoughts, feelings, and concerns honestly, we create a safe space for both parties to be heard and understood. This kind of dialogue builds trust, empathy, and ultimately, a stronger connection.

If you are tired of feeling invisible when you are with others and of not having the fortitude to assert yourself, let me validate that it's a horrible way to exist. It sucks to acquiesce to someone else to avoid upsetting them, and this pattern doesn't serve us as adults. If you struggle with this, I would guess that most—if not all—of your relationships are unfulfilling. If you keep silent and are afraid to show up as your true self, there is no way to have meaningful, fulfilling connections.

I recently had an experience where a person was verbally abusive to me. I realized that the pain I felt was old and familiar. When I was first triggered, I allowed my emotions to be there, then proceeded to calm myself down. Because I had been recovering from the pattern for some time, I was able to quickly set a boundary and let this person know it wasn't okay to treat me that way. But it certainly wasn't always like that. In the past, I would have remained silent and withheld my love. Most of the time, I would have felt a sharp pang of shame, as though I were being "put in my place."

There is no way for another to know what you want and need if you are afraid to speak up. The people in your life are not mind readers. If you are unhappy because your needs are not being met, it's up to you to ask for what you want or find a way to meet the need yourself. If you are afraid to speak up because you fear upsetting the other person or being rejected, this is where you need to take responsibility for healing your wounded child self. If you want to heal that pain from your past so you can feel worthy of love, the only way to do that is to go inward.

Conscious communication is key. When we speak

from our heart and not from our wounds, we discover that we are able to connect with each other in a deeper way. In order to unhook from debilitating patterns, we need to become aware of them and learn how they show up. What you think, feel, and desire matters. Assert yourself without being concerned that someone may leave you because you risked showing them who you are. If someone doesn't like when you assert yourself, it might be helpful to ask yourself whether you really want them in your life any longer.

DON'T BE AFRAID TO SHARE FROM YOUR HEART

I once found myself in a conflict with a loved one, and this conflict enabled me to identify a deeply ingrained pattern. I liken it to a dance that I engaged in much of my life, the people-pleaser dance: "Just be quiet and we will dance just fine."

If I spoke up and called a person out, they became angry. It was too painful for them to see that they were in the wrong, so they resorted to defending themselves by twisting my words and asserting *I* was in the wrong. Perhaps you've also tried to speak up and found that your truth mirrored those you were in conflict with. If it was too difficult for them to admit their imperfections, they may have turned the mirror around and said, "Look at your reflection—see how wrong you were?"

Nowadays, I don't dance that way. As I continue to

reparent myself, I realize more and more that I have the right to speak up and share what's true for me, even if others dislike what I have to say. My ability to confidently speak up for myself came gradually. It got to a point where I was simply no longer willing to tolerate the discomfort I felt when I resorted to silencing myself out of fear of being rejected. That pain of abandoning myself had become more difficult than the fear of being rejected.

It isn't always easy to speak up and share heartfelt feelings. In addition to worrying about being judged or rejected, we might blame ourselves for inciting conflict. According to renowned shame researcher Brené Brown, there is a difference between being judgmental and holding others accountable for their actions. Avoiding open communication only leads to further misunderstanding, hurt, and resentment. When we are willing to express ourselves without holding back, we give others an opportunity to face themselves and grow. We can then work together to find solutions and move toward a deeper understanding and appreciation of each other.

Not long ago, I had a conflict with my daughter. She was trying to find a part-time job to make extra money while studying for her master's degree. In my mind, I started telling myself a story that if she didn't get a job quickly, she was going to be broke. I believed she should take any job as long as she had money coming in. She had a different plan. We were discussing the pros and cons of various jobs, and with every suggestion I made, she resisted. I felt my anxiety and frustration increase and kept pressing her to see it my way and take my advice. Both of our emotions were escalating, and the situation became tense.

Finally, she said, "Mom, I appreciate your advice, but I'm feeling a lot of pressure from you, and I have to figure this out on my own." As soon as she said this, I paused and immediately reframed the way my mind was working. I took responsibility for the fact that I was operating out of an old, anxious pattern. I then apologized and acknowledged that she was right. From there, I changed my energy to one of simply listening and supporting.

The moral of this story is, since my daughter and I had been practicing conscious communication for some time, we were able to repair and remain connected to each other. Teaching my kids to communicate this way is one of my proudest achievements.

I encourage you to take the leap and start a dialogue with someone in your life you may have been hesitant to share yourself with. It takes courage to speak up, but the rewards are well worth it.

CULTIVATE HEALTHY COMMUNICATION

Throughout my life, whenever I've started a new relationship with a friend, I was mostly openhearted. The beginning of relationships, whether a friendship or romantic relationship, is exciting. You are getting to know one another, and usually are both on your best behavior. You think to yourself, "This person is wonderful," and you feel connected. But over time, this person perhaps falls off the pedestal you placed them on, because your expectations for how they should behave aren't met. You feel disillusioned.

This has happened to me countless times. I would meet someone new and feel connected, but as soon as she showed her imperfections by saying or doing something I deemed "wrong," I would struggle in the relationship, predominantly because I was too afraid to speak up for fear of upsetting her. Rather than take off my mask and speak honestly, I hid what I felt. I harbored those feelings and eventually withdrew, making excuses for why I couldn't get together for lunch or tea. I'd call less often until we talked only a couple of times a year. In time, the friendship simply fell by the wayside.

I told myself that I'd outgrown the relationship, but the truth was, I couldn't communicate effectively. Rather than discussing openly with my friend what I was feeling, I withheld my truth. It was easier and a familiar pattern not to rock the boat, so I remained silent about what I wanted and needed from the friendship. The problem with this way of relating was that I pushed away what I longed for, which was connection. Connection is vital for survival, and I was drowning in a lack of it.

Today, I actively cultivate healthy relationships by

speaking up more, setting boundaries when needed, and remaining true to myself. I am softening my armor to wake up my heart. As I learn to accept myself and my imperfections more and more, I am better able to accept the imperfections in others as well.

I have also come to realize that if I feel triggered by something another says or does and find myself judging, it's an opportunity to look into the mirror and explore where I might have the same behavior or quality within me. This provides a chance for me to accept whatever part of me I might be cutting off. Everyone and everything is an opportunity for growth, if we choose to see it that way.

There are still times when I choose to walk away from a relationship or keep space and distance. That's okay. Some people are not going to be as willing or able to reciprocate healthy communication. I call this practice "loving with a smart heart." Not every person in my life has to be in my inner circle, the place where I share my truest self with others, mask-free. But when I can communicate open-heartedly with those in my inner circle, it's the best feeling in the world. I feel seen and heard. And this is largely possible because I have learned to be more loving and accepting of myself. I see and listen to my wants and needs, whereas in the past, I ignored them. Like attracts like, which is why I now have people in my life who see me for who I truly am.

FIND BETTER WAYS TO RELATE

As much as I have tried to rescue my kids from uncomfortable situations or outcomes, I now realize that I don't have control over others. Pain is inevitable, and problems don't just vanish. Another pattern I had to practice unmasking from is trying to rescue my kids. It wasn't easy, but I'm learning to lovingly detach.

I encourage my kids that they can get through whatever life sends their way. And while that's happening, I can support them, but I can't save them. Whenever my daughter calls me and is upset, I listen and ask, "How can I best support you?" She then tells me if she just needs to vent or actually needs advice. This is different from all the times when I dove in and gave advice from the start. In the past, she felt I was trying to fix her, whereas now she feels that I am there to support her.

While I've accepted that I can't control the outcomes in my children's lives, I *can* plant seeds. Whether those seeds grow is not up to me. Wanting to help my daughter grow and heal from her own childhood wounds, I asked myself what I could do to water her inner garden and promote her ability to flourish. For starters, I knew that I had to find a different way to communicate with her. I needed to remind her of her true self. I also had to learn to look beneath her behaviors to identify her unmet needs. We all have unmet needs. It's the main reason we act out.

When she was a teenager, I decided one day that I

was going to have a heart-to-heart with her and asked her to set aside twenty minutes to really listen to me with an open heart. Seeking a better way of relating, I said, "You believe I don't understand you or what you are going through. I was a teenager once too. I know it feels like I only want to control and limit you. I felt this way myself at your age. You feel as if you have no choice other than to cut away from me. I get it, I really do."

It was clear that she was listening, so I went further. "To go forward, I ask you to share what you are thinking and feeling. Instead of leading with my agenda, I'm simply going to ask questions. If you can communicate your thought process, this will help me greatly. Show me how you will take care of yourself so that I can learn how to fully trust that you will be safe. Tell me everything you are thinking about regarding drinking, pot, sex, and driving with other teens."

It was an honest, difficult conversation to have, but oftentimes, the hardest conversations are the most needed. I needed to communicate clearly and directly with my daughter, and from that point, I had to ease my own anxieties about what would happen if I said yes to many of her requests so as not to upset her or cause friction. I had to check in with my gut and decide if I could offer a genuine yes when she asked permission to do something. And if my response was a hard no, I could explain why to help her understand where I was coming from.

CONNECTION BEFORE CORRECTION

One evening, my husband was yelling at our daughter, angry that she and her two friends were making too much noise in the basement. He was unhappy because, in response, she talked back and rolled her eyes. In such moments, we often feel a need to send our kids to their room or otherwise punish them, but this is counterproductive. What we need to do instead is connect with them instead of resorting to punishment. Punishment only addresses their masked behavior, not their true self.

We need to look beyond our kids' dysfunctional behavior to figure out what they really need. *We need to deepen our connection with our kids, not resort to correction.* Their behavior is just the outward sign of something brewing beneath the surface. My daughter rolling her eyes simply signaled that she wasn't present.

Over the years, I've learned that we can approach life from a place of lack and scarcity or with a sense of abundance. The key is to feel our inner abundance instead of focusing on what we imagine we lack. By focusing on our inner self, abundance spontaneously becomes the dominant theme. And if we want to come from a place of inner abundance instead of punishment, we need to focus on illuminating our children's inner selves. We do this, in part, by enabling them to feel good about themselves.

It took a long time for me to learn to speak to my children respectfully—to show them how competent and wise they are. At one point, I realized that my son was making some poor choices. It was crucial that I didn't reflect these choices by reinforcing them with my own dysfunctional patterns. He didn't need to be told he was behaving badly; he already knew. Instead, I needed to switch my focus to the root of his behavior, which lay in an unmet need.

I now realize that forcing kids to comply usually backfires. Imposing consequences is a poor way to get them to comply. They need to be allowed to suffer the natural consequences of their behavior, which can be hard to allow and watch.

My role is to guide them to make age-appropriate decisions on their own. If I want my children to have clear boundaries in their lives, I have to model for them how to do this, which isn't always easy.

My advice is, let your children make their own way, with you by their side. What our kids need isn't a perfect parent, it's a loving one, one who is increasingly becoming more real alongside them.

When they were learning to walk, our children needed to find their own feet. We were alongside them, of course, but they had to stand up and learn to place one foot ahead of the other. This is still how (metaphorically speaking), now that they are in their twenties, my kids are still developing the ability to trust themselves. As counterintuitive as it may sound, being powerless over our children *is* powerful.

I see more clearly than ever that I can't rescue my kids from discomfort. It's their job to learn to rely on themselves—to find the inner strength and knowledge that, no matter what happens, they can get through difficult situations. Like me, they can learn to calm themselves in the storms of life. I know that I am equipped to support them, but I can't fix their issues or put a pillow underneath them to break their falls.

As a parent, this has been one of the most difficult things for me to do. To this day, I fight with myself because I want to swoop in and rescue my kids, make everything as easy as possible for them. I hate it when they struggle and are in pain. On the other hand, I realize that pain and struggle is what will help them grow—just as the caterpillar needs to struggle through the chrysalis stage if it is to become a butterfly.

Rather than looking at what they are doing wrong, I choose to see *their* gold. I have learned to see that they too are part of the ocean, not just the waves. They are good and worthy simply because they were born, and it's important for me to trust that they have what they need to get through life.

There came a point when I sensed that my childhood self was quieting down because she was feeling more confident that my adult self would be there to provide safety and reassurance that she could get through hard things. Tired of fighting her way through traffic, she was confidently giving up her need to drive the bus, allowing my adult self to take the wheel so she could live in a more relaxed manner. Consequently, I am able to relax and trust that my children can get through hard things. They are strong and self-reliant.

BECOME UNATTACHED WITHOUT BECOMING DETACHED

In order to have meaningful relationships, it's important to learn how to be independent. Too often, we are either too attached or too avoidant, both of which can leave us feeling miserable and empty.

Relationships help to remind us that if we are either too commingled or too separate, we can't deeply relate, heart-to-heart. We will no longer honor our true feelings or value another as a person in their own right instead of solely for how he or she makes us feel.

As I mentioned earlier, when my husband and I first met, he showered me with attention. I became attached and dependent on him to continue to make me feel special. When the newness of the relationship wore off, however, he stopped buying me roses every day (as one would), and suddenly, I no longer felt special. I didn't feel the same closeness. It is also important to note that when I was angry, I would oscillate and become detached. I would give my husband the silent treatment until I was ready to move forward. This was classic codependent behavior I learned from my mom.

I have witnessed in my relationship with my

husband as well as in others' relationships that one or both partners are often attached to the idea that the other needs to show up in a particular way. The wife or girlfriend may pressure her partner to be more emotionally available, while the husband or partner may want to be more physically or sexually connected. This was true of my relationship. The problem is, we're too attached to the idea of the other being the way we want them to be. This puts tremendous pressure on the relationship, and oftentimes, one or both begin to feel resentful. Instead of feeling connected, we feel separate and, many times, lonely. Because many of us don't want to leave our relationships, we double down on trying to make the other person change. Remember what I have been saying all along: "We can't change other people, we can only change how we respond."

To be close while being fully ourselves necessitates being *unattached* without becoming *detached*. Being *de*tached derails a relationship, because failing to engage can cause us to drift apart. To be *un*attached, on the other hand, is to be deeply involved in a relationship without losing ourselves or those we care about. Being unattached brings out more of ourselves *and* more of the other, and it's what freed me to be my true self in the presence of others.

I've learned that another great privilege is to witness who another truly is––to be so connected and yet so individualized that we can fully rejoice in the "otherness" of those we care about. To be who we are *and* to assist another in being who they are is one of the most rewarding experiences life has to offer.

However, if we are merged with another—whether a spouse, parent, child, friend, or group—we risk losing that which caused them to be interested in us in the first place. No one can care deeply for someone who, over the years, has diminished themselves to the point that they are a nonperson. Relationships are meant to develop us, not encourage us to lose ourselves in another.

It took a long time for me to realize that I had lost myself in the role of mother, wife, and daughter. It was no surprise when I did a podcast interview with guest Dena Farash, titled "Why Moms Are Miserable: What To Do About It," that I deeply resonated with her story. Dena was honest and vulnerable, sharing that she at times hated being a mom. She was a stay-at-home mom, and unlike some mothers who actually love the role of being mom, Dena did not. She admitted that there was a time when she couldn't wait until her husband got home from work just so she could go to the grocery store for half an hour, alone. She struggled to stay connected to her true self. I admired her confession on how much guilt she carried about wanting to escape from her kids and the role of mom. She verbalized what so many moms feel but are too afraid to admit.

Not only can we become attached to others but we

can also become overly attached to the need to have things go our way, which can also give us a sense of powerlessness.

In order for me to further my growth, I had to learn to accept life exactly as it is in any given moment, without attaching to an alternate desired outcome. For such a long time, I resisted accepting the way things were. I would repeatedly ask, "Why is this happening to me?" I remember Dr. Shefali's words from one of her courses: "You can't expect the sky to be orange when the sky is blue." In other words, you can't change people, places and things. Learn to accept. One of my favorite prayers is The Serenity Prayer: "God grant me the serenity to accept the things I cannot change, courage to change the things I can, and the wisdom to know the difference." This prayer helps me remember that I have to accept things as they are and let go of my attachment to things going a certain way.

I learned how healthy and serene it feels to accept and let go. To be unattached but not detached. Everything that happens in my life plays a part in my evolution, and for that reason, I don't need to know the future. I don't need to know today whether I will eventually go back to work, open a wellness center, or host retreats. So why drive myself crazy trying to figure the future out? The key is to surrender to each moment as it arises.

When people speak of surrender, they assume they are supposed to surrender to their situation, which is the opposite of taking charge of their lives. It doesn't occur to most of us that we are being asked to surrender to something *within* ourselves—something that's asking to stand up and be recognized.

As our masks dissipate, we are each asked to embrace the powerful individual we are. We awaken to the incredible person who's been hiding beneath our masks. This is fundamentally different from capitulating to our circumstances, and the result is that we no longer absent-mindedly float downstream.

Don't surrender your preferences, the things that really matter to you. Instead, embrace them. Reflect your true self with its capacity to intend the very best for you and everyone who matters to you. Step out of your smallness and into your greatness.

If you have bought into the belief that things are "meant" or "not meant" to happen, let me refer you to the words of Professor Stephen Hawking: "I have noticed that even people who claim everything is predetermined and that we can do nothing to change it, look before they cross the road."

Getting Comfortable Setting Boundaries

If you struggle with people-pleasing tendencies and want real change in your life, it's important to cultivate a practice of setting and holding boundaries. Over the past few years, I've learned a lot about setting boundaries and cutting the energetic cords that led me to feel that I'm "not enough." I also deliver a resounding "no thank you" to the guilt and shame that often follow the setting of boundaries.

A while back, I attended a retreat outside my comfort zone with the intention of leaning into my discomfort by doing things I'm not comfortable with. I was uncomfortable going due to the type of people I assumed would be attending with me (who I suspected were far more uninhibited than I am), coupled with the exercises, which I knew would be a bit too touchy-feely for me. The retreat strongly hit on my intimacy wound.

The first activity we were asked to do was stare into the eyes of a stranger for a few minutes. Those few minutes felt like hours, and I was wildly uncomfortable. It was the first exercise we were asked to participate in, so it felt even more difficult to back away from doing it. At that moment, I wasn't ready to assert myself by opting out.

As the retreat continued, we were asked to engage in more activities, and they became increasingly uncomfortable. This was when something began to shift in me. I started asking myself whether the real test for me wasn't to push myself into doing things that didn't feel right, but to speak up for myself. During one of the activities, I told my partner that I couldn't continue to go through with the exercise. I was incredibly nervous telling her, because it would leave her without a partner, and more so, the leaders would be aware that I wasn't participating. Thankfully, my partner understood and respected my boundaries. I slipped out the door and went back to my cabin. The truth is, no one else even noticed that I stepped out. It was the exact healing I needed.

On the last day of the retreat, some of us spoke to the group of eighty people, sharing our experiences. I chose to speak, and I admitted that at the beginning of the retreat, I was judging them for being weird and "out there." But as the weekend went on, I realized that we were all the same, and the real issue was that I was afraid to set boundaries. I realized that I didn't have to be like them, hugging all the time and crying in public. I could say yes to what felt right and no to what didn't. This was a huge breakthrough. It was evident that the healing work I had been doing for so long was paying off.

FINDING FREEDOM TO SAY NO

It can sometimes be difficult to know when we are saying yes in order to squash the pain of saying no. This is especially true when we are so busy that we don't take time to pause and notice what's going on within us.

Do you spend time with family members when you don't want to? If so, what would happen if you said no? How would they respond?

For many years, my mom hosted a cookie exchange with my cousins and aunts. I really didn't want to go to these get-togethers. It wasn't that I didn't enjoy my cousins and my aunts, because I did. But I wasn't into making cookies and participating in the tradition. I also felt like I didn't have a choice.

Well into my twenties, I still felt that I couldn't say no to my mother. Whenever I tried to back out, she presented me with the newest guilt trip. I became the queen of making all sorts of excuses for the odd times I did say no. Eventually, I found the courage to say that I wasn't going to attend the annual cookie exchange, and she stopped pressuring me. But it took time to heal and move through the guilt and fear I felt for so long when saying no to her. Once I learned to deliver a firm no, however, I regained control of myself.

The ultimate test happened when my mom was nearing the end of her life. Both of my parents had major health issues in their later years. They suffered from varying degrees of dementia, heart issues, and debilitating arthritis, among other things. They could no longer take care of themselves without assistance. My sister took care of their bills, and I assisted with their healthcare.

They needed day-to-day help, and while my cousin, who lived nearby, did his best to help when he could, they needed more. The issue was, my mom resisted paying for help. She had an expectation that I would take care of her and my dad. It was a generational belief that she held, given that she was my grandmother's primary caretaker.

My mom was pretty sick the summer before she died. She ended up in the hospital for a while and needed more care when she got home. Once again, I pleaded with her to allow me to hire a health aide to come to the house and take care of her and my dad. She fought me, because she wanted me to take care of them.

This was an absolute no for me. I had two kids of my own as well as my own health issues to manage. I was more than happy to make the arrangements to hire help, but I wasn't willing to physically be her caretaker.

I know this broke my mom's heart. She saw it as a sign that I didn't love her or care about her, which of course was far from the truth. I loved her enough to want to get her the help she needed. Money wasn't an issue; the issue was that she wanted me to be there with her more often than I could be.

We fought a lot that summer, and I had to firmly stand my ground. I'd worked hard to heal from my past wounds of feeling like a failure as a daughter and the limiting belief that I wasn't enough for my mom.

While I was in turmoil, feeling horribly guilty, I also realized that I had to stand up for myself once and for all. I'm glad I did, because she passed away six months later. Had I not allowed myself to be an adult with her that summer, I wouldn't have had the opportunity to heal the unhealthy patterns between us. I've healed so much generational crap through my relationship with my mom, including decades of people-pleasing tendencies.

Whenever another decides to meet our needs, it should be freely given. And if the answer isn't a full-body yes, one should have the freedom to say no without guilt. An individual with a strong sense of self doesn't get offended and take it personally if another denies a request.

This is the main reason I never forced my kids to do things for me out of a sense of obligation. I never wanted them to experience the feeling of being forced to do things for others. If I asked for a favor, I always prefaced it with "You don't have to do this if you don't want to." It was important to me not to continue the pattern of guilt tripping to get what I wanted.

KNOWING WHEN IT'S MOST IMPORTANT TO SAY YES

How long has it been since you said yes to someone or something in your life, even to yourself? When opportunities come your way, whether personal, spiritual, or work-related, are you overly cautious? Do you shy away from opportunity?

When I was in the throes of people-pleasing, I shied away from opportunities, mostly because I wasn't accustomed to having my wants, needs, and desires fulfilled. Sometimes, we learn to say no so well that it becomes just another pattern. We may even feel we don't deserve to say yes to ourselves, but learning to say yes is as important for our growth as is setting boundaries.

For a long time, I denied myself opportunities that seemed expensive. Since I was a stay-at-home mom, I had a belief that our money was really my husband's money. I believed that because he earned it, it was more his than mine. It didn't matter that I brought value to the family and supported him while he grew his business. It also didn't matter (in my mind) that in the state of New York, fifty percent of what is "his" would be mine if we divorced. I couldn't allow myself to feel worthy or deserving of making big financial decisions.

For a long time, whenever we went on vacation, I would only get a massage if he suggested it. I tended to wait for his permission to allow myself to indulge. It's not like he forbade me from enjoying myself. It was my own ingrained belief, one that I brought into the relationship.

Several years back, I finally said yes to an incredible opportunity to go to a spa weekend at an exclusive, retreat center. I had heard about this place from others and wanted to go for a long time. We had the money available, but I wouldn't allow myself the opportunity. Until, that is, I finally pulled the trigger and went for a weekend with my daughter. It was difficult to give myself permission, but I pushed through the discomfort I felt and booked the trip. The idea of spending quality time with my daughter helped push me over the edge because it was more about us than just about me. In addition, I didn't want to pass on the pattern of denying myself opportunities because I felt unworthy. It felt great to finally say yes to myself, even though I still felt a bit guilty. This was a new behavior for me, and it took a lot of self-coaching and persuading from my daughter to get to that yes.

My daughter was a great mirror for me when it came to learning to say yes to myself. She has a belief that she is worthy and entitled to having nice things—

on Mom's dime, of course! This was evident when, about a year ago, she asked if we could go to Italy. This was a trip that, in several ways, pushed well beyond my comfort zone.

I wanted to practice being open to receiving and feeling deserving of saying yes. Even though I had been experiencing a luxurious lifestyle for a long time, I never felt fully deserving of it. The childhood wound that I wasn't worthy enough ran that deep. While I sat in my lay-down first-class seat, I intentionally practiced feeling worthy of receiving. Eventually, I was able to lean into feeling grateful for the abundance I was experiencing, a feeling that seemed so natural for my daughter.

Another reason I shied away from saying yes to opportunities was that, as a perfectionist, I was accustomed to playing small and didn't take many risks for fear of messing up. I was used to my husband planning our trips and knowing that if something went wrong, he would handle it. I never had to worry. However, our trip to Italy had many moving parts. There were several flights with tight connections, and I arranged for drivers to pick us up at precise times so we could make those connections. We made every one without a hitch, and every driver was on time and cordial. We had only one driver who didn't speak great English, but somehow, we still communicated.

Another concern I had about traveling without my husband involved my health issues. Throughout the trip, I continued to worry, because I have fears when it comes to being away from my own doctors and landing in a foreign hospital. I said to myself throughout the trip, "I need to stay in the moment." In order to help my child self feel safe and secure, I had to remind myself repeatedly that, no matter what happened, I would be able to make good decisions and handle whatever arose.

My daughter and I made a pact that we would do our best to remain calm and relaxed. We would flow with whatever happened in each moment. She used the phrase "straight chillin'," continuously declaring we were "straight chillin'."

Part of the expansion from that trip came from taking the risk so I could test my ability to handle any mishaps along the way. Because I was determined to grow and step outside my comfort zone in order to grow, I believed I was rewarded by a trip that went seamlessly. In fact, we also lucked out with the weather. The week before we went, Italy was experiencing unusual cold and rain. In addition, one of the volcanoes in Taormina had erupted just days before we arrived. I'm not proclaiming that things will always go our way just because we take a risk, but I do believe that we can manifest more of what we want when we're aligned with a more positive mindset.

This trip expanded my horizons beyond what I expected. It's experiences like this that have stretched me. I felt free and empowered, having grown enough to say yes to this opportunity, not to mention how wonderful it was to experience life's abundance with my daughter.

Being True to Yourself

It's easy to have a hard time knowing how to avoid being submerged in the dynamics of family, groups, or our place of worship, all of which can cause us to lose what's unique about us and take on another's identity (merging). But if you want to have a fulfilling life of joy, abundance, peace, and freedom, you must learn to trust yourself. If you look outside yourself, hoping for others to tell you how you should live your life, you will undoubtedly feel lost.

My desire to belong was so strong that I repeatedly lost myself, becoming submerged in various groups. One such group was a place of worship I belonged to many years ago. Because my sense of self was weak back then, I was drawn in by the pastor's charisma. I wasn't adept at thinking for myself, and I adopted beliefs that didn't feel true to me. I joined a Bible study group, attended worship each and every Sunday, and volunteered. I was even baptized and accepted Jesus Christ as my savior.

The problem was that deep down, this was not for me. I actually felt worse about myself—and somewhat brainwashed. I don't regret that I went to this church, because every experience that's occurred in my life has been a learning opportunity. But I learned how to set a boundary for myself, and in due course walked away. I became stronger just by standing up for myself, knowing what was right for me and what wasn't.

There have been many other times throughout my life when I've looked to others for answers on how I should live my life. I didn't have a strong identity or strong convictions and was easily swayed by others. I read books, attended seminars, and watched programs hosted by experts, especially on the topics of health and parenting. I often heard them speak on a topic and told myself excitedly, "That's the key to what I'm working on!" However, in the long term, none of it worked. Life was leading me to see that the answer lay within myself.

I have learned that I can read or hear something and simply take it into consideration, without treating it as "something I must do." I don't need to look outside myself to books, pastors, groups, or therapists to tell me who I am, although several helped me get to this point. Part of taking radical responsibility for creating the life you desire is learning to think for yourself and not be swayed by others' opinions. True freedom is having a strong sense of self that can't be shaken.

TRUSTING YOUR INTUITION

In the spirit of learning how to better trust ourselves, it's important that I touch upon the importance of trusting our intuition. How can we recognize when our intuition is speaking to us? And how can we trust what it's saying?

As a child, I was told again and again that I was "wrong" about what I thought, felt, or believed. Because this was drummed into my head, I learned not to trust myself. This lack of trust led me to be terrible at making decisions. While organized religion isn't for me, I do appreciate a specific Hebrew scripture. Elijah is told to stand on the mountain to which he has journeyed. Once he gets there, drama begins. First, there's a wind—perhaps a tornado or hurricane—so powerful that it splits rocks apart. Following the windstorm, there's an earthquake. After the earthquake comes a firestorm, likely a fireworks-level display of lightning. During none of these events does God appear to Elijah. Humans have long tended to associate God with dramatic events in nature, but the message of this story is that showing up in the midst of dramatic events isn't how the infinite presence that undergirds the universe makes itself known to us.

Only when the drama is over does Elijah perceive God's presence, which the traditional translation describes as "a still, small voice." More modern versions render this expression as "a gentle whisper" or "a sound of sheer silence." The expression "a sound of sheer silence" points to the absolute stillness of our inner being. It's a peacefulness, a stillness that's much deeper than anything we can think or talk ourselves into. It's the reason we need to ignore what we *think* we know and step into stillness as we tune into our intuition. It *is* our intuition.

This sense of peace is different from the kind of enforced mental and emotional peace brought about by suppressing our thoughts. It's a bedrock state that's always present within us and that we can tap into whenever we choose.

This kind of sheer silence is palpable. It's the stillness we experience when we become one with a sunset, transported out of our mundane state by the rapture of the moment. It's the stillness we feel when afloat the vastness of the ocean. It's the silence of a night sky ablaze with galaxies, when we are in the wilderness, away from all artificial light. It's that utterly hushed stillness we experience when walking in a snow-covered winter wonderland. It's the stillness I experienced as a child on the water at my aunt and uncle's lake house.

Quite the opposite from urging us in one direction or another—the way contradictory voices in our head and impulsive emotions do—this stillness will never force itself on us. It will only make its presence known in the background, giving us the opportunity to respond if we so choose.

I was put to the ultimate test, having to make one of the biggest decisions in my life, when my mom had a cardiac event nine days prior to her passing. She was on life support for those final nine days, and they were some of the hardest days of my life. The doctors and nurses kept reassuring my sister and me that my mom could pull through. Several times, they reduced her Fentanyl dosage to wake her in order to ensure that she had brain activity. Each time, she had a look of sheer fear and panic in her eyes, at which point I begged the nurses to increase the medication and let her go back to sleep.

The concern the doctors had was whether or not my mom would be able to breathe on her own. They allowed her to attempt to do so on two separate occasions during those nine days. Each time she failed, so they re-intubated her. A critical decision was coming down the pipeline. My mom could not breathe on her own, and the doctors still were not convinced of what caused the cardiac event in the first place.

One option was to do surgery and give my mom a tracheotomy, then send her to a nursing home she might never leave. My dad was still alive, but he was already suffering from dementia and wasn't able to take care of her. The other option was to give my mom a third and last try to breathe on her own. If she couldn't, we would let nature take its course with the assistance of drugs to keep her comfortable.

This is where I was put to the test. The decision to keep her alive or let her go was too difficult for my sister, so I made it. When the nurses started to wean my mother off the Fentanyl and she was alert, I spoke to her and told her that this was the last attempt to let her breathe on her own. I told her I would not let her suffer anymore. Going to a nursing home was not an option for my mom as far as I was concerned. I reassured her that I loved her and that she was a good mom. I knew she had done her best to raise us. I told her that if she wasn't able to breathe on her own, she could go on her way. She passed away later that day.

As sad as I was to lose her, I was at peace because I had an inner knowing that it was the best decision for her. I was also at peace because I knew I had healed the patterns and negative energy between us.

During those last days of her life, I was able to connect with her on a spirit-to-spirit level, as a human being, not as a wounded child. I was there consoling her and reassuring her that I loved her. Although she couldn't speak, I could see in her eyes that what was once between us had healed. She spoke clearly with those eyes, and to this day, when I look up at the sky and see clouds, I can see a formation of a face with clear, defined eyes. I know in my heart that it's my mom's way of letting me know she's there.

It was the adult part of me that was present with my mom, and it was this part that was capable of making such a monumental decision. I knew why it had to be me and not my sister making this decision—it would be a huge part of my healing. Whenever I reflect on my mom now, I feel nothing but love and acceptance for her. I have no anger or resentment for the way my childhood shaped me. I know now that my life was designed to play out exactly the way it did, to shape me to be the person who is able to write this book.

I can't say that I have had that inner knowing and peace with all of my decisions, but I know that when I tap into my intuition, I feel peace. When I resist listening to my intuition and try to force solutions or outcomes, I experience a lot more suffering. The saying "That which we resist, persists" is true.

When learning to trust your intuition, start out small. Try driving down a road you haven't taken before. Try a new coffee shop that intrigues you or eat a new food you've been wondering about. From there, you might try making bigger decisions such as redoing a room in your house while trusting your intuition to help you choose paint colors, exploring a new hobby, or perhaps making a new friend. Such things will enable you to become more attuned to your intuitive feelings, eventually becoming adept at letting this aspect of yourself guide you.

ALIGNING WITH YOUR INTUITION

When my children were five and two, prior to being diagnosed with Sjogren's, I'd been sick for a long time. In fact, I'd begun to notice that something wasn't right after the birth of my first child. The doctors assured me that it was normal to feel the way I did after giving birth, especially since I hemorrhaged during delivery. I continued to go to different doctors for mysterious symptoms, each time being told I was normal and healthy. This only contributed to the confusion I felt. No one believed me, and I started to question myself. Since I was in the habit of listening to others rather than listening to myself, I believed the doctors more than my symptoms and accepted that what I was going through must just be part of the healing process after giving birth.

About a year later, when I still felt like an eighty-year-old in a thirty-year-old's body, my gut continued to tell me something wasn't right, even though others were practically declaring that I was crazy or a hypochondriac. Even my husband didn't fully believe me. He started calling me "Horizontal Kimmy," because I was always on the couch. It was painful that even he didn't believe me. I knew in my heart that I wasn't exaggerating about how sick I felt, but my husband making these kinds of sarcastic comments only further reinforced my self-doubt. I was angry that he wasn't more understanding and supportive. I needed him to hold me and reassure me that I would be alright.

The struggle continued when I had my second child. I was very sick during that pregnancy. I also had preeclampsia, and because my blood pressure was dangerously high, I was induced five weeks early. I hemorrhaged again during delivery. The horror story continued when I hemorrhaged again two weeks postpartum while at home. It would be another three years before I'd finally receive a diagnosis.

I felt isolated and alone in those days without anyone supporting me with my concerns. I was worried that I had cancer and was convinced (again) that I was going to die. These feelings may have been exaggerated because of that time I swallowed the pine needle—it's amazing how much trauma a tiny pine needle can inflict!

It was bittersweet when I finally received Sjogren's diagnosis. On one hand, I had to learn to manage a chronic illness that has no cure, but on the other hand, I was glad I could prove to my husband and all the others that they were wrong. I wanted to shout, "See, you didn't believe me, but I knew I was right."

Where in your life have you ignored what you know to be true? Maybe you know you're in an unhealthy relationship, but you override that "knowing." Perhaps you are stuck in a dead-end job, knowing you are supposed to be doing something different with your life, but others continue to admonish you to stay where you are.

If you are ignoring something you know to be true in your heart, I encourage you to listen to yourself and trust your intuition. This is how you align with it. Any time that quiet, still voice is talking to you, trust it.

Opportunities to Grow

Given my experience as a teacher, I believe that only when we grow in wisdom are we really getting an education for life. Wisdom comes from our personal experiences. It isn't how much we know, it's what we do with what we know. It isn't what knowledge has been stored in our heads, it's how we *use* our heads.

Wisdom enables us to process what we experience so we can derive insight from those experiences. For this to happen, we need to be present in our experiences. People who grow in wisdom aren't easily hoodwinked by their emotions, the deceptiveness of the situations they encounter, the machinations and manipulations of others, or the inarguable craziness of society. Wise people use everything they experience as an opportunity to develop their ability to discriminate between what's beneficial and what's harmful.

Do you spend too much time focusing on the circumstances of your life instead of the lessons? Believe me, I know how easy it is to get caught up in *why* things are happening to us. Many times, I focused too heavily on the problems in my life, particularly my relationships. But focusing on the problem sends me into a spiral where I end up once again in a victim mentality, stuck in a mindset of lack and scarcity.

Instead, I increasingly practice looking to see how events and circumstances can help me grow myself up. Once I learned to look at circumstances as opportunities to grow, I began to see them as tools for learning, which catapulted me out of victim mode. I learned to feel the pain I was going through, which led to healing. Whenever something feels "off" or a pattern shows itself, I have learned to be compassionate with myself. Instead of asking why adverse situations occur, I ask what the lesson is.

What problem or circumstance have you been focused on in your life lately? Does it make you feel like a victim? Can you, just for today, contemplate what the lesson might be? As the poet John Keats said, "Even a proverb is no proverb to you till your life has illustrated it." The acid test of any piece of wisdom is whether it has become bedrock to our way of *being*.

Rumi also encouraged us to welcome opportunities to grow:

This being human is a guest house.
Every morning a new arrival.

A joy, a depression, a meanness,
Some momentary awareness comes
as an unexpected visitor.
Welcome and entertain them all!
The dark thought, the shame, the malice,
meet them at the door laughing,
and invite them in.
Be grateful for whoever comes,
because each has been sent
as a guide from beyond.

When we look at all of life's experiences as an education for life, we can view it as a journey toward the wholehearted embracing of all that makes up our lives. It requires opening our channels of desire full throttle until we are taking in life's richest experience in the fullest, most wholesome way.

PART VI

MY MESS IS MY MESSAGE

Spreading My Message

As a result of all the work I've done on myself, I developed a need to express to others what my journey has taught me so far. As I pondered how to do this, I recognized that I needed to do something that *truly* interested me—to think outside the box that once imprisoned me. I didn't want to go back to work at a job that didn't fit me. I wanted the kind of work that didn't feel like work but was instead an expression of my creativity, an outpouring of the person I now find myself to be. I needed to be immersed in work that came naturally to me.

On my podcast, which I started in May 2020, I speak with experts, reasoning that these conversations could help so many who struggle with backgrounds similar to my own. Connecting with my guests by having heart-to-heart conversations feels natural to me—like playing on the monkey bars. I also write regular newsletters, and I look forward to speaking on stage. However, if I'm being honest, until recently there was still something holding me back from "being all in." I suspect there was still a remnant of imposter syndrome, a fear that I didn't have what it would take to have a wildly successful podcast or to write a book—even though my intuition absolutely told me to continue pursuing both. My heart and soul knew that this book needed to be birthed, even though a part of me continued to tell me I was crazy for taking off my mask and being naked in front of the world.

Growing up, what mattered most was always the outcome, so that's what always defined me. My worth was dependent on my grades, my achievements in sports, the number on the scale, how many friends I had, and, later in life, how much money I had. I was afraid that if I couldn't achieve the outcome I thought I *should* have (followers, likes, downloads, and readers), then who was I to put myself out there to be Snow White?

During meditation one day, I realized that my self-doubt was protecting me from putting myself out into the world. My mask told me that if I went for it, I would be disappointed and feel rejected. I was tempted once again to stay safe by playing small. It occurred to me that this was the old Kim's way of approaching life. It taunted, "Don't put yourself out there—don't go into the arena."

But if I continued to focus on the old Kim and the

ways she fell short, I would inevitably feel defeated. If I exhibited a defeatist mindset, I would end up asking myself, "Why bother?" If I quit seeking to share myself—and part of me wanted to—I would pass this generational pattern to my kids.

Furthermore, I feared that if I came to the end of my life without leaning into this knowledge, without aligning with my intuition, I would regret that I didn't push harder to share what I have learned. Now, I focus on my commitment to serve others. I know this message of teaching others to become aware of the masks they wear and how to unmask in order to be their true selves is crucial. And it's especially important to educate our teens and young adults on how to live mask-free to have a more fulfilling life.

This led me to come up with the idea to talk in schools, spreading awareness about the dangers of wearing masks. Not only do I have six years of teaching under my belt, but I've also raised two kids and am well-experienced in my own healing journey around mask-wearing. From the time I started my teaching career at the age of twenty-three, I wanted to change the entire educational system. I never believed or supported standardized testing, and I didn't feel that kids were learning what they needed in order to thrive.

Growing up, we receive an education centered around passing information from teacher to pupil, but we don't necessarily get many courses focused on living. We might learn how to *earn* a living, but this doesn't mean we have learned how to truly live. We may have a lot of know-how but that doesn't necessarily mean that we are wise.

Our culture places emphasis on IQ, grades, and testing. But when it comes to enabling ourselves and our children to create a fulfilling life, IQ, grades, and test scores count for far less than society gives them credit for.

We don't want to stuff knowledge in people's heads, least of all our children's. We want each of them to mine their own depths. We want our kids to discover within themselves a self-confidence that's foundational to who they are. This will equip them to weigh the ideas and opinions of others but not be controlled by them, to consider the input of their peers but not feel they have to fit in, and to listen to everyone but let their course of action come from the deep well of their own being.

Back when I was teaching English, I taught "at risk" kids. The very fact that they had been given this label provided them with a mask they could put on if they so chose. But I saw my students for who they were and didn't judge them based on whether they were failing or getting into trouble or doing drugs. I didn't even read my students' files when I received them. I simply connected with them and saw their true selves.

Because I could see who they were behind their masks, they gravitated toward me. They wanted to be around me and connect with me. They knew I was not judging them and accepted them for who they were. I created a safe space for them.

I did something most teachers didn't do, especially teachers of "at risk" students. I would call their parents and share something positive about their child, showing them the gold within them. When I phoned parents to give them an update, they were shocked to hear a good report. I highlighted their child's accomplishments instead of addressing any failures. Some parents actually thought I'd made a mistake and was calling about another student!

As a result of my experience as a teacher, witnessing students put on masks, coupled with my own experience living in suffering because I was afraid to be my true self, it has become my mission to help parents become aware of the masks that both they and their children are wearing and the impact it is having in both cases. I'm passionate about helping teens and young adults remove their masks in order to be their true selves and have a more fulfilling life.

In order to help teens and young adults be their true selves and remove their masks, it is important to understand what most strongly underpins the issue today. In her book, *Never Enough,* Jenny Wallace discusses how today's children and teens are under increasing pressure to excel in all areas of life—academics, athletics, extracurricular activities—often at the cost of their mental health.

When I was in high school, there were days I went

to school all day long, then to soccer practice, then to marching band practice before getting home at ten o'clock, only to start my homework. I remember throwing myself on the kitchen floor in a fit of tears over how overwhelmed I felt. The internal pressure to perform, to be perfect and productive, stayed with me. I found myself constantly fighting, not to be a human "doing" but rather a human *being*. But it wasn't easy to rid myself of the sense that if I wasn't being productive, I didn't matter.

In one of the episodes of my Masks Off podcast, I spoke with Dr. Eric Recker about toxic overachievement and grind culture. He shared how he also spent much of his life striving to be perfect, always "grinding it out." It's become yet another epidemic among today's youth, driven by what Jenny Wallace traces to the root of this grind culture: the fact that we feel we "don't matter."

Mattering is essential for all humans. It's why we are conditioned from day one to believe that unless we are productive, preferably excelling, we aren't valuable. It's why I would override my body every time it was telling me to slow down. Rather than pay attention to my body, mind, and spirit when it was exhausted and depleted, I pushed onward. So many of us have this mindset, and it's very unhealthy.

We need to take time to recharge and nourish ourselves in order to be more productive. I am currently taking an online course with Mel Robbins, and one of the lessons is on mindfulness. She teaches that research shows that when we are more mindful, we have better focus, better memory, we are less stressed, and we have more clarity in our lives. She therefore suggests that we do ten-minute mindfulness activities each day. Mel adds that many of the most successful people have a solid mindfulness practice. The irony is that many of the course participants are overachievers, and many of them are resisting the mindfulness activities because they feel it's too easy. Imagine that!

One of my podcast guests, Holly Swenson, shared this quote with me from Dr. Sukhraj Dhillon: "You should sit in meditation for twenty minutes every day—unless you're too busy; then you should sit for an hour." Do you feel like you are lazy if you slow down? Do you have a part of you that is driving you to "do" all the time? Do you have a part of you that screams, "You are a nobody if you slow down"?

I want to reiterate that I am not suggesting that you abandon your responsibilities. I am inviting you to look at the energy that you bring to the things you do throughout the day. Can you reframe the way you view the tasks you have to do and see them as opportunities rather than feeling enslaved by all that you do? Can you infuse your day with mini mindfulness breaks? If you aren't experienced or familiar with mindfulness, consider taking a course or searching online. Rather than feeling overwhelmed by all that you have on your plate, can you focus on one step at a time while being present?

If we are going to create a paradigm shift away from the toxic grind culture, we have to be willing to be aware of the signs and the impact it has on us and the future generation. I'm passionate about helping to spread awareness of the dangers of perpetuating this kind of toxic overachievement, which is based on intense competition instead of cooperation. I imagine a day when school children are given the message that it's their birthright to know who they truly are. But in order for them to understand that, *we* first have to understand it. It is my belief that if we do the inner healing work, we will be free to be our true selves. We won't feel the need to protect ourselves by wearing masks. This is true freedom.

True Freedom

Maurice Chevalier, French singer and actor, explained, "If you wait for the perfect moment when all is safe and assured, it may never arrive. Mountains will not be climbed, races won, or lasting happiness achieved."

Perhaps you tell yourself that you are waiting for just the right moment to start a new career, leave your marriage, get in shape, or write that book that you've always wanted to write. I too often put off the things I wanted to do for myself until the "right" time. So many times, I said that when the kids were older, I would travel more by myself. When the kids were out of high school, I would do whatever was in my heart. When they were older, I'd focus on healthy eating and working out.

But these were just excuses. I was sitting on the sidelines, waiting for the perfect moment to start living my life. The problem is, all we really have is this moment. We are not guaranteed tomorrow. So why wait for the "perfect" time? What *is* the perfect time, anyway?

You can choose to wait until that "someday" arrives, or you can choose to live your life as it unfolds, day by day. Is there a dream hidden inside you, something you've wanted to do for so long you've almost forgotten what it was? Maybe you want to go back to college, get in shape, start a podcast, or travel to some exotic place. Whatever it is, you might make a wish list and write down three to five things you dream of doing. Choose one thing on that list that has been quietly waiting for the time to be right. Then begin to take steps to make your dream happen.

Look in the mirror for a few moments. Instead of simply being honest with yourself about what you see, be honest with yourself about what you "believe" about the reflection staring back at you. There is a difference between what we believe about ourselves and who we really are. Do you harbor beliefs that keep you from showing up fully and authentically in your relationships? Do you have beliefs that you aren't good enough to go for that job, that business venture, or that new relationship? Do you have beliefs about being a failure, causing you to play small in the world?

I have a dream to be on Mel Robbins' podcast and Lewis Howes' School of Greatness podcast. My energy used to be that I wasn't worthy enough to be on their podcasts, which, to my way of thinking, stemmed from all the way back when I was turned down for the lead role in "Snow White." I made a decision to heal this pattern once and for all, to both remove and bury the masks holding me back. The timing was perfect, because it was on my front burner.

After all, if I wanted to be a freedom fighter to help liberate others, I needed to break free from the fear that kept *me* playing small. It had always seemed as if this pain had been caused by people and events on the outside, but what I learned was that it arose from inside myself. Therefore, I had the power to both claim and remove it.

It took time and much soul searching, but I eventually had a monumental shift in how I saw myself. I finally knew my worth and value beyond the shadow of doubt and became able to exist unapologetically as my true self. While I have not been invited to be on Mel Robbins' or Lewis Howes' podcasts yet, I have no doubt that I could hold my own with either.

Speaking of Mel Robbins, she was recently a guest on Jay Shetty's podcast. He asked her if there was something she was presently "struggling" with, and she replied, somewhat surprisingly, "Happiness." Jay was as surprised as, I can only assume, many listeners. Had she kept her mask on, she might have said, "Not much!" After all, that's what people perhaps assume of her, having written and spoken so much about her own growth. But her transparency made her so much more relatable, because, in truth, the journey doesn't end. It only evolves.

In the spirit of taking off my mask and being completely transparent, there are a couple of patterns/belief systems I'm currently working through. It's also important and a great way to concretely show how I use my POWER Pathway to work through my own leading edges of discomfort.

I have a block when it comes to receiving money from clients. While I have a desire to have a thriving business, whether that includes one-to-one coaching, speaking, or both, I'm struggling with self-doubt and my worthiness to receive money.

I know exactly where the pattern comes from and have alluded to it throughout this book. The beliefs I created from being turned down to play Snow White, told I couldn't play forward in soccer, and advised not to apply to a reputable college because I wasn't good enough to get in, are still ingrained in me. Not to mention, my husband's voice is chirping in the back of my mind, saying, "Why are you doing this coaching thing anyway? It's a saturated market and you won't shine through all the 'noise,' so why bother? What I've repeatedly heard is that I'm not good enough or capable enough to achieve a desired outcome.

The other pattern rearing its head and preventing me from charging a fair hourly rate is the belief that I will waste our money. If I invest money in this business—or in myself, for that matter—by hiring a producer for my podcast or someone to build an online course for me and it completely flops, then I've wasted our money (or, in my mind, my husband's money). He's made comments in the past about some of my choices, such as investing in online courses, attending retreats, or getting certified in hypnosis, stating that, in his opinion, it was a waste of money.

Here's how I've managed it in order to grow through it and take the people-pleasing mask off in this case. First, I got hyper focused on the pattern and where my limiting belief originated. Next, I owned that if I wanted to change this pattern, I needed to be the one to heal it. I don't need to blame my husband, my mom, or all the people who doubted me in the past. I then repeatedly nurtured my wounded child self, because she's the one who feels she isn't good enough. From this place, I began to challenge my belief systems and start taking small steps toward creating the life that I want, which includes having a successful business where I feel worthy to receive money.

THE JOURNEY NEVER ENDS

"Psychology Today" relates the story of the night before the Buddha became enlightened, when he fought a great battle with Mara, who attacked him with lust, greed, anger, and doubt. Even after the Buddha became revered throughout India, Mara continued to make unexpected appearances. Instead of ignoring Mara or driving him away, the Buddha calmly acknowledged his presence, saying, "I see you, Mara." He would then invite him for tea and serve him as an honored guest. Offering Mara a cushion so that he could sit comfortably, the Buddha filled two earthen cups with tea, placed them on the low table between them, and only then took his own seat.

We all have a shadow side of ourselves that we need to own up to, an aspect of ourselves we wish we could shed, an aspect we hide by putting on a mask. Being willing to "have tea with Mara" means we aren't afraid to witness these dark parts of ourselves.

When I find myself comparing myself to others and becoming envious, I could beat myself up, or I could say, "Let's have tea, Mara." By doing the latter, I become willing to *include* the aspects of myself that compare and feel envy.

I can say with certainty that the only way to become a fully integrated person is to confront head-on whatever lies ahead of us in this never-ending journey. Continuing to make big leaps in my personal growth and stepping outside my comfort zone is the prescription that allows me to be free to be myself. I embody the belief that I am enough, no matter what the outside looks like. There is nothing on the outside—no person, thing, or situation—that can make me feel unworthy or unlovable. As this truth becomes more solidified in every fiber of my being, there is no reason to fear stepping out into my light and being my true self. I have such freedom in knowing that I am ok and will be ok no matter what. I want this for you too—to feel so self-assured that you no longer can be shaken at your core.

Said Bulgarian-born Maria Popova, an American essayist, author, poet, and writer of literary and arts commentary, "Every once in the bluest moon, if you are lucky, you encounter someone with such powerful and generous light in their eyes that they rekindle the lost light within you and return it magnified; someone whose calm, kind, steady gaze penetrates the very center of your being and, refusing to look away from even the most shadowy parts of you, falls upon you like a benediction."

My hope and wish for you is that you feel inspired by my journey of going from "prison" to "paradise," inspired to take a long, honest look at the patterns you are living. Then to make a conscious, committed decision to do the inner work to heal your pain and embrace every part of your being. Remind yourself repeatedly that you are the ocean, you are divine, and you matter.

Do not allow anyone or anything to detract from your "knowing" that you are worthy of being your true self at *all times*. Trust that you are unshakeable! When life gets hard, because it will, know that you are capable of doing hard things. Pain is inevitable, but suffering is optional. It is possible to live a life free from suffering. It is possible to have inner peace, joy, freedom, and abundance. You can reclaim your inner power and feel empowered in everything you do.

You may still be a bit skeptical about what I'm saying, and I get it. There was a time when I didn't believe it either. But I kept persevering and finally reached a point where my life began to gradually shift. Yours can too!

ACKNOWLEDGEMENTS

I am forever grateful for my kids and husband. Without you, I wouldn't have had the opportunity to grow into the woman I am today.

To my loving parents, who I miss so much.

Dr. Shefali, it was no coincidence that you entered my life when you did. My relationship with my kids would not be what it is today without learning about Conscious parenting.

To the many coaches and therapists who guided me along the way, you helped make the journey more tolerable and I could not have done it without your support.

To David Robert Ord, I'm amazed by how you took such raw material from my journals and crafted it into a work of art. You are an amazing wordsmith.

And finally, to Elizabeth Lyons, my editor and publisher, thank you for the numerous times you pulled me from falling off the cliff. You were amazing at finessing my work and guiding me to turn this book into something that I am so proud of. I can't thank you enough.

www.ingramcontent.com/pod-product-compliance
Lightning Source LLC
Chambersburg PA
CBHW020457030426
42337CB00011B/140